Other books by this author include: *Storming Heaven with Prayer for Healing and Deliverance*

Coming soon: *Storming Heaven with Prayer for America and the Nations*

For Restoration and Breakthrough

Storming Heaven
— with —
Prayer
Book II

ARDITH BLUMENTHAL

WESTBOW
PRESS®
A DIVISION OF THOMAS NELSON
& ZONDERVAN

WestBow Press books may be ordered through booksellers or by contacting:

WestBow Press
A Division of Thomas Nelson & Zondervan
1663 Liberty Drive
Bloomington, IN 47403
www.westbowpress.com
1 (866) 928-1240

ISBN: 978-1-9736-9741-1 (sc)
ISBN: 978-1-9736-9742-8 (hc)
ISBN: 978-1-9736-9740-4 (e)

Library of Congress Control Number: 2020913702

Print information available on the last page.

WestBow Press rev. date: 07/28/2020

With whom will you compare me? Who is My equal? asks the Holy One. Look up into the heavens! Who created all these stars? As a shepherd leads his sheep, calling each by its pet name, and counts them to see that none are lost or strayed, so God does with stars and planets! O Jacob, O Israel, how can you say that the Lord doesn't see your troubles and isn't being fair? Don't you yet understand? Don't you know by now that the everlasting God, the Creator of the farthest parts of the earth, never grows faint or weary? No one can fathom the depths of His understanding. He gives power to the tired and worn out, and strength to the weak. Even the youths shall be exhausted, and the young men will all give up. But they that wait upon the Lord shall renew their strength. They shall mount up with wings like eagles; they shall run and not be weary: they shall walk and not faint. __Isaiah 41: 26-31(TLB)

Contents

Dedication

This book is dedicated to my late sister who always inspired me to be better than I am. She believed in me when no one else did and prayed for me when everyone else had given up. She inspired me to take on this assignment because she never lost sight of her own coming restoration. She found no case a hopeless one, not even hers, and always believed the best of people. She tended the soul of every wounded or needy friend or stranger along her path. She maintained her optimism and sincere belief that God was working all things for good, even in the face of insurmountable odds. She left us a legacy of hope that the power of love is indeed stronger than death.

Preface

When I was a little girl I used to complain bitterly to my Dad about having to do chores in the barn. I remember crying and telling him "It isn't fair." His answer was always the same; "Nobody said life would be fair, sissy." I found it infuriating. But, as is often the case with parents, he was right. Life isn't fair. You don't have to make it very far along the path before you meet that truth head on. Whether injustices are intentional or accidental they hurt. I'm not talking about the injustices sending people scurrying to safe spaces. I'm talking about injustices like my classmate getting a tennis court for her thirteenth birthday and everyone else getting a cake for theirs. I'm talking about my brother dying of a deadly disease before he was forty while other's brothers are alive and well. I'm talking about my friend who was paralyzed in a car accident and then received a cancer diagnosis just for good measure. These deep injustices change one. When something hugely unfair, tragic or terrible happens it can cause one to change the way one sees and engages life. These events can completely bleed us of our resources or "empty our bucket" and we find ourselves in search of a place to replenish, a place to be restored. Restoration is what I address in this book; the restoration of broken and lost human beings. Brokenness comes in all sizes and shapes and every degree of severity.

On several of our mission trips abroad our team has worked with newborn infants discarded in garbage heaps, under buildings, or lying exposed in the baking sun. We rescued them, tended them, treated them, and felt overwhelmed with grief because we had to leave them in shelters and orphanages without knowing what life-long scars they will bear from being so utterly discarded and unwanted. These children were totally innocent and yet abandoned when most vulnerable and helpless. Thankfully, most of us don't experience such violent rejection or need such complete intervention and restoration. But, most of us do know what it feels like to be hurt when we are our most exposed and vulnerable.

I've learned a great deal about the pain and disappointment people face. Some of this learning came about from my own life story, and some of it was learned through the suffering of others. When you work in healthcare or travel to serve the poorest of the poor, you witness many stories of pain and loss.

We only have to listen to the news for one hour to discover the extent of tragedy and incomprehensible devastation some face. In the news just today, there was an earthquake in Turkey, an explosion in Houston, and a plane crash in Afghanistan. In each instance lives were lost or shattered. We know refugees in camps around the world are reeling from loss and want. Thousands around the world are displaced, hungry, ill, living in conflict zones or in extreme poverty. In my experience, every encounter with trauma and loss creates a need for recovery and restoration. Certainly there are degrees of tragedy and admittedly some handle difficult situations better than others. But, as far as I can tell, people rarely make it through the events of life unmarred or unscathed by pain and loss.

This book came about because of what I personally saw happen to a friend. He didn't encounter ISIS, he wasn't wounded in war, nor did he get thrown out of his home. Many actually looked at him and thought he had a charmed life, full of all the good things money could provide. I know other people who appear to have suffered greater losses than he. Even so, when he finally requested help he was in dire straights. He actually called my husband, a longtime friend, and said, "I hear your wife is a woman of God and I need help. Would you bring her and come to see me." It was the day after Christmas when we first sat down to talk about what was going on. He was unaccustomed to asking for help, or talking about God, so it was really uncomfortable for him.

Suffice it to say, he'd been through the ringer. He'd had a bout with cancer, he'd lost his fortune, he'd lost his family, his children weren't speaking to him, and worse, were being turned into his enemies. He was considering bankruptcy. He didn't really know God, though he knew of God. In addition to his cancer diagnosis, he was severely depressed and emotionally and physically depleted. He felt joyless, vulnerable and lonely. He'd grown up going to church and attended religious schools for his entire education. Still, he was tentative about the God of the Bible. He just knew he needed divine intervention. He knew stories from the Bible, but because of corruption in the religious system. He'd determined the God he'd learned about wasn't a God he liked much. The true and living God had been misrepresented by a religious system that enslaved him as a child and ignored and annoyed him as an adult.

There was a certain mystery regarding how he'd arrived at his current position of loss and pain. It snuck up on him and devastated him like some kind of malevolent fog. Now, wrecked, he was forced to look outside himself for something or someone to bring him back. When he asked for Godly help I knew he was serious about seeking the real solution. I learned from our meeting that all the other pathways to a solution had been blocked. Nothing he tried was effective. In fact things just kept going from bad to worse. As it is with most of us, God was his last resort. Humans seem to be like that. We turn to God after the mess is made. Thankfully, God is not really the last resort, but He is always the best resort.

It turned out to be an honor to pray for him and go to war for the return of what the enemy of his soul had stolen. His brokenness seemed to remove his resistance and he accepted our prayers with humility. Not once did he try to mandate or control us or tell us what He wanted us to pray.

We formed a small group of praying friends who we knew would be faithful and agree in prayer regarding his needs. We determined to pray until there were measurable results. It took time and strategy. The prayers in this book worked for him. After several months of our group praying for him he began to say the prayers aloud over himself. As he grew to know and trust God, his fear and loneliness began to dissipate. His health improved, his children began speaking to him, a way to make a living appeared, and court cases began to settle in his favor. We were witnesses to the Almighty intervening in his life. He's still a work in progress: things are much improved, but not perfect.

If you have suffered loss and pain then God wants to restore you as well. He wants to return to your possession those things stolen away by the enemy. "For I know the plans I have for you, declares the Lord, plans to prosper you and not to harm you, plans to give you hope and a future" (Jeremiah 29:11 NIV). He wants you to focus on Him and discover the destiny He has in mind for you. He wants only good for you. You can trust Him for everything you need.

It's true there are lots of prayers in this book. It's true we had to persist for a number of months before we saw changes actually take root. Sometimes, according to scripture, we must "Ask and keep on asking and it will be given to you; seek and keep on seeking and you will find; knock and keep on knocking and the door will be opened to you" (Matthew 7:7 AMP). We have to be like the persistent man described in the parable from Luke; who pounded at the gate until his sleeping neighbor got up out of bed and gave him the bread he sought. We too, must be persistent until God responds to our asking, seeking, and knocking.

Some fights are hard won, and this was one of those fights. We simply persisted until the prayers were answered with a

"Yes." and an "Amen" (2 Corinthians 1:20 KJV). The name used in these prayers has been changed to the name of my late father, Doug, and the situations generalized to protect any real persons.

At the moment, I'm actually praying these prayers over a friend. Her case is totally different than Doug's case. She needs physical restoration from the after-effects of chemotherapy. I change names and situations to fit her need and pray aloud with her every day. The prayers are helping her so much. I encourage you to do the same.

Acknowledgements

Thanks to my husband and editor extraordinaire for all the time, advice, and patience he always affords me. It's such an honor to have you on my side. Thanks to those who prayed along with me for this miracle of restoration and breakthrough and who cared so deeply for the welfare of a stranger. Each of you truly is the "Good Samaritan" Jesus spoke about. Thank you, Karen, for help in referencing the scripture behind each prayer. I love you all

Introduction

While you and I can be, and often are, blown about by the winds of change and the pressures of life, the Word of God doesn't change. "Forever, O Lord, Your Word is firmly fixed in the heavens" (Psalm 119:89 KJV). This means His promises, all of them, are available to you and me. What He does for one, He will do for others. "Then Peter began to speak: 'I now realize how true it is that God does not show favoritism but welcomes those from every nation who fear Him and do what is right' (Acts 10:34 NIV). When He promises to restore us or win a battle for us it's a promise upon which we can rely.

When the enduring nature of God's Word comes to my mind, I often think about the Jewish people who were exiled and separated from the land of Israel for two millennia. All that time, through trials, through pogroms, through persecution, peril, and sword, they believed the land of Israel would be restored to them. At Passover, they would say, "next year in Jerusalem." Now, after two thousand years, Jerusalem is restored to them. Why? It's because God made a promise for their restoration and God is true to His Word.

> Thus saith the Lord of hosts; Behold, I will save my people from the east country, and from the west country, and I will bring them, and they shall dwell in the midst of Jerusalem; and they shall be

my people and I will be their God, in truth and in righteousness.

Zechariah 8:7-8 (*KJV*)

God has demonstrated His nature by showing us His power and desire to call us home and restore us. He longs to be reconciled with each of us and return into our possession those things the enemy has taken from us.

There is an amazing story in the Old Testament regarding restoration. King David, a King of ancient Israel, was engaged in a battle, and on the third day of the battle he and his soldiers returned home to the city of Ziklag. David, and his men discovered "all the women of the place and those who were there from small to great had been carried away into captivity by the Amalekites" (1 Samuel 30:2 KJV). They found the city burned to the ground and nothing and no one remained. David's entire company was extremely distressed and they wept long and bitterly and his men even wanted to stone him as they held him responsible for the tragedy, David, whose wives and children had also been taken captive, strengthened himself in the Lord, and inquired of the Lord, saying "Shall I pursue this troop? Shall I overtake them?" and He answered him, "pursue, for you shall surely overtake them and without fail recover all" (1 Samuel 30:1:8 KJV).

The place was burned to the ground. There was absolutely nothing left except empty smoking ruins. You or I may have given up and blamed God but David did not. He already knew beyond question that God was on his side and what that meant. After seeking God and receiving authority from Him, "they recovered alive each and every man, woman and child, and all the plunder. Not one thing was missing and David brought everything back" (1 Samuel 30:19-20 KJV). What complete restoration! He recovered all that was lost and was reunited with his family, his people and his material possessions. This is the power of God. David sought God, believed God, and acted on his God given authority, and all was restored. That same principle is at work right now for you.

The prayers in this book are prayers for restoration and breakthrough. They are personal; prayed on behalf of a dear friend who suffered great tragedy and loss. It seemed like it could be too late as, like David, he'd already lost everything. He was stripped of his business, his health, his family, his fortune and his self respect. He'd reached a point where he realized that he was out of resources. He was empty in the physical realm and empty in the spiritual realm. He'd exhausted every legal avenue, spoken with friends and counselors, tried to solve his problems his own way and now was seeking to find a God who is alive and real and active. He was suffering from acute depression and severe loneliness. He was shattered. Like Job, he'd done nothing wrong. He was a pillar in his community, a successful businessman, a generous philanthropist, and a ready volunteer for others in trouble or need. His children were his greatest hope and joy. Nothing any longer made sense to him. How could it? He was innocent and yet found himself desolated. He needed someone to step into the trenches and fight his battle with him. He needed an emergency rescue squad to engage the enemy and force the return of what belonged to him.

When we are sick, frightened, alone, and in pain it can be impossible to fight on our own behalf. We need someone to come along and pull us out of the hole we are in and pray us into an upright position. Once we've spent all our own capital we sometimes have to rely on the capital of others. This was such a case. King David's story is compelling evidence, we too, can have assurance that God will make it possible to recover those things and people stolen from us. Just as God did for King David, when you ask Him, He will help you reclaim and restore what's been stolen from you.

Because I want you to experience the passion of the prayers, I maintained them in the first-person but have used my late father's name. I have used italics to highlight a paraphrase of scripture, followed by the citation of scripture from which it was taken. They are all derived from scripture and they speak God's promises and Word back to Him. Pray one each day and pray them aloud. When we pray in this way we know God hears us. "God is watching over His Word, (or keeping watch over His Word), to fulfill or perform it" (Jeremiah 1:12 AMP). Since He has bound Himself to His promises and His Word, we can trust He will hear and answer our prayers.

Chapter One
I am Not Forsaken

Though I walk in the midst of trouble You preserve my life: You stretch out Your hand against the anger of my foes; with Your right hand You save me.

—Psalm 138:7 (AMP)

The Lord will perfect that which concerns me. Your mercy, O Lord, endures forever; do not forsake the work of Your hands.

—Psalm 138:8 (NKJV)

I was standing in the emergency department when the ambulance pulled in. The patient was critically injured. Bones were broken, blood pressure crashed, breathing shallow; death being held at bay by the youth of the victim and quickly acting paramedics. The medical team sprang into action. We needed skill, speed, and resources from every department. We had to pull out all the stops if we were going to reverse the damage and restore this young man to his family. The injuries, damage, pain, and urgent nature of our task was obvious to all of us. The unconscious patient was the only one unaware of the peril he was facing. Without intervention, death was imminent. Even with the best outcome, recovery and restoration were months away. This is a true and graphic example of a pivotal moment that occurs in most every life.

The situation may vary, but there seems to be a moment where one is faced with situations or circumstances that, without an emergency intervention, are insurmountable. We might not know it at first. We may think it will all be okay. We are more or less unaware that we've reached critical mass and have passed the point of no return. Then suddenly, we find ourselves unable to navigate. We are simply powerless to conquer the problem pile. Life has become overwhelming; the choices too difficult and our strength too small. We are out of options, out of energy, out of money, and out on a limb. With resources exhausted, we come to the end of ourselves. We must either seek help or end up being taken away by the flood of circumstances sweeping through our lives. Granted, not everyone faces the same types of emergency. Some people are like the frog that starts out in cold water. Things heat up one degree at a time until it's too hot to handle. Others may face financial, relationship, or health issues. Families collapse, natural disasters occur, houses catch fire, cancer strikes, and people die. The big question is: How does one get over, through, under, or around this pile? Then how do you repair the damage, manage the fallout, recover, and move on? Who's in charge of emergency relief, recovery, and restoration?

We can all think of some answers to that question, right? The answer might be shrinks, doctors, friends, insurance companies, or winning lotto numbers. But seriously, if you live through it, how do you pick up the pieces and move past it? In Western society we are taught to be responsible. We are supposed to take care of ourselves, stand on our own two feet, and pay our own way. We are encouraged to make our own decisions and to be self-actualized. I, for one, pursued those goals with enthusiasm. That's why I always tell people I learned everything the hard way. If there was a mistake to be made, I made it. I was in full pursuit of "the dream." I chased down opportunity and angled to be in the winning position, whatever the prize or price. It was many heartaches and heart breaks later I became aware that what I saw as my mandate was the opposite of God's mandate.

I'd been raised in a religious home by parents who genuinely loved me and who were motivated to serve God and to see that I served God too. Independence, self-reliance, problem-solving, and hard work—these were all important family values, and they were reinforced in all our activities at home, in school, and in church. We knew we had to get the job done. These survival skills were built into our understanding of everything, including our definition of what God expected—or demanded—of us. Unfortunately, they represented a false religious narrative.

God never said, "Do it on your own." He never asked us to decide what would be right. Acting independently came after the Fall. Separated from God and cut off from the garden, humans were rightly determined to survive. For the first time, people were forced to make their own decisions. Those decisions, unfortunately, led to the destruction of the entire human race, except for Noah and his family. We weren't exactly great at doing the right thing on our own.

When God revealed Himself to Abraham and chose the Hebrew

nation as His own, He promised good to them in exchange for devotion and obedience. He revealed to them their need to depend on Him totally. He showed how serious He was when He provided the law to Moses. He gave them a written code of ethics and appeared to them in the form of a pillar of fire by night and a pillar of cloud by day. God directed everything, even the daily activities of the entire nation. Yes, they had freewill. They could be, and often were, disobedient; but God's mandate, given to Moses through the Torah, was a requirement for His blessing. The Torah provided a law for every aspect of life. No decision was left to chance. If they wanted the blessings of God, then they had to follow the requirements. Humans shortly proved themselves pretty uniformly unable to follow what God required. It caused a lot of trouble! For the Jews it was forty years in the wilderness, for starters. It turned out the dependence God was asking of the Israelites was nearly impossible to achieve. Human nature balked against the idea of this performance-based acceptance. It was clear that grace was going to be required.

Prior to the resurrection of Jesus, the Gentiles didn't even have the opportunity to access the true God. The Living God was God of the Hebrews only. It was Jesus, (Yeshua, in Hebrew) who changed everything. He reconciled mankind with the Creator, restored us to the possibility of fellowship with the Father, and brought us back into intimacy with God. God knows how our independence caused us such deep grief, endless disappointment, and great longing. His intent all along was to make us totally dependent on Him because our restoration is intrinsically linked with dependence.

> Then Jesus answered and said to them, Most assuredly, I say to you, the Son can do nothing of Himself, but what He sees the Father do; for whatever He does, the Son also does in like manner.
>
> (John 5:19 *NIV*)

"I don't speak on my own authority. The Father who sent me has commanded me what to say and how to say it" (John 12:49 *NIV*).

I often meditate on these scriptures, thinking how much more we, than He, require instruction regarding our words and actions. We were never designed for, nor intended to follow, the dictates of our own unredeemed minds. We were designed to be connected to God and conformed to His design and plan for us. This is a tough concept because it is so foreign to our understanding of a meaningful life. God says He knows best. He knows who you were designed to be. He chose a path for you. He planned for you to fulfill your divine destiny. It is our choices, pride, and stubborn behavior that keep us from being truly fulfilled and joyful. They are also the qualities that cause us to get in trouble in the first place. We may not know it, though, because most of us have never learned the truth about independence.

We are spiritual beings living in frail, perishable vessels of blood and bone. We can never be fulfilled until we are filled with, and under the direction of, the Holy Spirit. "Those who are in the realm of the flesh cannot please God" (Romans 8:8 NIV). We have a higher calling. We are intended for, actually born for, the purposes of God. Yeshua/Jesus makes it clear that we are not meant to be on our own and can't really expect much if we are separated from Him. "I am the vine; you are the branches. If you remain in me and I in you, you will bear much fruit; *apart from me you can do nothing*" (John 15:5 NIV; emphasis added).

For me, this caused a very big internal fight. I can assure you with everything inside me that I never once considered giving up *my* life or personal goals for a life an invisible God supposedly designed for me. That was taking things too far. First of all, it was my life, wasn't it? God talking to people at all, much less calling me to a life of service, was definitely not for me. I had plans, dreams, a big future imagined for myself and those around me. I was smart, ambitious, and indomitable. I was proud to be called strong-willed. When others felt God was speaking to them about their lives I was vaguely amused and certainly relieved He wasn't talking to me. My determination for self-realization and achievement made it easy for the world to pull my young and impressionable heart toward material success and the false premise that I was in charge of my own destiny. It didn't take that much to be lured away from my upbringing.

At first I told myself I was being independent, just like God wanted. I embraced the world and set about to conquer it with a sort of cooperative God who, as always, sat at the distant sideline waiting until I had an emergency or disaster for which I might need help. Anything other than that only placed restrictions on enjoying myself. I broke all the rules that surrounded me as a child. I found them restrictive and unnecessary. God seemed more myth than in charge of anything. He certainly had never done anything for me personally, as far as I could tell.

It seems, even though I all but forgot about God and tried to put Him and His plan on the sideline, He didn't forget about me. He didn't try to stop me from making my own choices but I now know that He was with me the entire time. He allowed me to make a mess of my life all on my own and boy did I! I made one bad decision after another. I went deeper and deeper into the world system and away from my upbringing. I thought things were going great, but before I was thirty-five, I'd used up every external and internal resource I had. I found myself flat on the floor looking eye to eye with my own limitations. It was then, after I'd lost everything: my house, my business, my friends, that, like the prodigal, I found myself turning to the God of my parents for help. There was no other place for me to go to fill the bucket I'd emptied out. I'd tried it all and nothing had worked. I wasn't big enough to fill the cavernous hole I'd made in my own heart; I was utterly and totally broken. All I could do was cry. I'm not exaggerating. I could hardly remember my own name. I wasn't on drugs, I wasn't drunk, I wasn't bound for jail; it wasn't like that. It was worse. I could feel the pain, every last drop of it. I had not one good decision to my credit from the day I walked away from God. I didn't feel there could be enough mercy in heaven for me.

At the time, I was thinking about the prodigal from the pig sty, but I was more of a smashed to pieces earthen vessel. Everything inside me had evaporated, leaving me utterly empty. The extent of the shattering was complete. I told a friend it was like someone had dropped a light bulb from a vast height to the concrete floor below. The shattering was as fine as powder. I learned first hand how God gives us permission to break His laws, but the consequence of breaking them leads to being broken as well. "His Word is forever settled in the heavens" (Psalm 119: 89-96 KJV). No amount of pushing against it cancels or annuls it. It stays in effect like the law of gravity.

When I crawled back to God I didn't really want to. I simply could think of no other way to survive. I knew from the difficult situations my parents survived that God alone was capable of saving my life.

He looked at my misery with kindness, love, and mercy. He picked up all those tiny shattered and powdery pieces of blood and bone and began to create a vessel to his liking. I didn't want to face the process of recovery or restoration. I wanted to find a dark hole and never again see the light of day. But God is patient, loving, and merciful. He waited. If I lay in bed staring at the wall, He was with me. He didn't say a thing. He just kept working over hours and days and months. I was so incapacitated. The repairing seemed hopeless. I was of no use to anyone. I might have been able to go through the motions of living, but my heart was still broken, my mind sick and depressed. I went forward because I had to. I had a child who depended on me. God waited. There was no word of condemnation, no word of judgment, no suggestions for self improvement or change. He was just there, watching over me.

It wasn't a sudden miracle. It was a day by day mending. There were no shortcuts. When my strength began to return I once again showed my true colors and sidestepped and resisted committing my life fully to God. I wanted a convenient belief. I didn't want anything radical to happen to me ever again. I wanted an easy life I could understand. It seemed like there were too many failed challenges to ever need another. I'd paid a high enough price so I just wanted middle ground. Every time I tried to choose neutrality the path was a blocked and I would have to turn around. I still wanted my own way. I was asking to be made whole, but only on my own terms. My vision of wholeness didn't want to wait on God's plan. I wanted the destiny I saw for myself, not the plans and purposes of God.

Surely He would never require me to do anything I didn't want to do? Didn't He know what I'd been through? This caused many delays because I was fighting against my own restoration.

When I agreed to pray for my friend and his restoration I knew what he was asking. I knew what it means to have nothing left. I knew why He needed help standing up again and why it would take time and lots of praying. These great traumas in our lives, whether the happen in one moment, or over time, bend and break us. It takes time to heal, time to rebuild, and time to restore lost hope.

Chapter Two

He will Revive Me

Though I walk in the midst of trouble, You will revive me; You will stretch forth Your hand against the wrath of my enemies, and Your right hand will save me.

__Psalm 138:7 *(NIV)*

Throughout time the themes of restoration and transformation have populated the stories of one culture after another. From the Odyssey, to the Bible, to fairy tales like Cinderella, humankind is always seeking someone or something to reveal to themselves and others who they really are. Somehow we miss the chance or lose it or are afraid to let the truth be known. Sometime or somewhere bits of us were taken, captured, lost or wasted. We experience rejection, gossip, violence, anger, and false accusations. It hurts. Tragedy strikes. Love is lost; dreams lay in ruin, or worse, just beyond our grasp. Others do not "see us," and we can so easily lose sight of the person we know we are, or at least, should have been. Expectations we have of ourselves coupled with those others heap on us can push us away from our essential essence. Bad choices may have obstructed us or taken us on an unfamiliar path. Even good choices sometimes encounter insurmountable obstacles. We've been disappointed by others who made promises they didn't keep. Others don't live up to what we saw in them. Health fades, people grow old, loved ones are taken from us.

It's no wonder we long for something to fix our broken hearts. The world seems harsher than it should be. It's hard to figure out who is on our side, or if anybody is. We long to return to something beautiful and fair. We need a hero to come along and save us, transform us or somehow change our story.

We often try to change our situation by "managing" our way out of it. Perhaps we break up our relationships, divorce or move. We switch jobs, go back to school, drop out of school, or pick a new social network. We see the plastic surgeon and long for a time when we will look different, feel different, or stop feeling altogether. While these things may be a fix for the short term, they actually fix nothing. They may move us out of, or away from, imminent danger and put us in a different set of circumstances, but they don't fix any of our broken parts. We can shop until we drop, work until we fall over, hide out of sight, reinvent ourselves over and over, and yet the pain of our brokenness settles deeper and deeper into our core. The people around us, even those we are closest to, don't see us. No one seems to notice we are broken. Friends and family expect us to behave toward them in the same way we always have. They don't seem to notice we are all beat up. We say to ourselves, "If only I had a different family, if only I felt better, had more money, looked younger, were in a loving relationship, had children, didn't have children." You get my drift. When it boils down to the nitty-gritty, we are pretty powerless to fix ourselves without outside help. We long for change but even when we try our best we easily slip back to old patterns and habits. We know we are working with flawed materials.

The world can be a very unforgiving, violent and unjust place. Nations are raging and political positions are always at odds. There are wars, refugees and criminals. We have personal trials ranging from unpleasantness to tragedy so extreme recovery seems impossible. Usually we can put the negatives behind us and move forward to the next thing. Sometimes though, we meet storms we cannot weather. These cataclysmic events don't just mold us; they break us and bring us to our knees and sometimes to our faces. They challenge our identities and sometimes forever alter the way we perceive ourselves, our lives, and our relationships. Going forward seems impossible when just standing up takes all the strength we have. Where is the real hero we've been waiting for? Does such an intervening hero really exist? He does. He rescued me and He can rescue you. Who is He?

I propose Yeshua/Jesus is that hero. From the wedding in Cana (the place where, according to the Bible, Jesus performed His very first miracle), we have an example of how He can take something and transform it into another thing altogether. He took a stone jar which held water for the guests at the wedding to use for washing their hands and feet. There was nothing special about the vessel and the water was not for drinking, but for washing. He had the servants of the household fill the jars with water and instructed that they be filled to the brim. Once they were filled to the brim with water, Jesus transformed them to vessels full of fine wine. "We are but earthen vessels" (2 Corinthians, 4:7 KJV). He showed us through this story that He has the power to completely restore us, though we are ordinary run of the mill human beings, He is fully capable of transforming us back to our original design. He wants us to be what He intended from the beginning; something wise, and loving, something kind and true, and something filled with joy. The size, shape, color, condition and design of our vessel are a matter of little importance to God. He wants to mold and mend us until we can be filled all the way to the brim. Once we are whole and as He designed us, He will return us to being carriers of His grace, glory, mercy and kindness and restore us to the life He designed us to have.

Chapter Three
I Can Depend on God

The sum of Your Word is truth (the full meaning of all Your precepts) and every one of Your righteous ordinances endures forever.

___Psalm 119:160 *(AMP)*

Life is cumulative. It's an amalgamation of events and circumstances compounding one upon the other. People, schools, jobs, families and situations have a commonality, but to each individual, every experience is unique. This collection of data and how it's perceived by the individual comprises a large part of what we believe to be true. It informs our opinions of others, and to a very large degree, our opinions of ourselves. I call those opinions "individual truth." It is this concept of individual truth that defines our present culture. We hear people say things like "find your truth,' "my truth is" all the time. This mind set makes truth subjective and malleable. By definition, truth is a verified, indisputable fact. It is not a feeling or a hunch and it doesn't change just because one wants it to.

In reality, much, if not all, of what we think of as truth is actually factually incorrect. On the contrary, it is often an out and out falsehood. As an example, my husband is a very smart guy. He missed one question on his SAT's, was a National Merit Scholar Finalist, and has a high IQ score. But guess what? His father treated him like he was worthless and stupid. Those scores and awards mean nothing to my husband to this day. He is still, in some visceral way, defined by what his father said about him. The facts have been unsuccessful in blotting out the deeply seated and hurtful lies presented to him as truth by his own father. The Bible says the devil is the father of all lies. It says there is *no truth* in him. The father of lies is busy every moment trying to convince us that we are bad, ugly, stupid, irresponsible; you name it. It's only in understanding and believing what our real Father, the God of the Bible, says about us, that we can be restored. The source of truth is God. "The sum of Your Word is truth (the full meaning of all Your precepts) and every one of Your righteous ordinances endures forever" (Psalm 119:160 AMP). When we believe what our heavenly Father says about us it brings with it the freedom only found in truth. We must search for the bedrock of truth. Finding and facing truth is the only way we can be restored and set free from the perils of the present and the pain of our past. Being whole doesn't come from medicine, although medicine can remove symptoms; it doesn't come with counseling, although counseling may help. Wholeness comes when we accept and believe the truth about our real identity. We were with God *before* the creation of the world. (Ephesians 1:4 KJV e*mphasis added*). He is our Father and His purpose and intent do not expire. He is always at work on our behalf. He wants us to have the best possible life. He put each one of us here for this time. We are his children and heirs to all His promises. We have gained both an eternal and an earthly inheritance (See *Ephesians 1:1-23 AMP*).

You were placed in your earthly family for a reason. You are where you are for a reason. God's reasoning is vastly superior to ours. He knows why you are where you are. He knows what his plans and purposes for you are. "The plans of man are many but it is God's plan that will prevail" (Proverbs 19:21 NIV). The further we are away from God's plan for our lives, the greater the wreckage we can create. *When we acknowledge Him, He directs our paths and on that path we will find restoration and wholeness* (Proverbs 3:6 KJV).

Longing is a human condition. We were born into a world where we don't feel at home. In past years, I loved being in my garden. It was so satisfying to plant seeds and to help my plants grow, bloom, and thrive. In the mornings I would rush to my garden with coffee in hand so I could snip off dead flowers or pull out weeds. It was such a satisfaction. I realized at some point that within each of us there is a longing to be in the garden. It was the first stop for mankind, and we all have an innate longing to return to the place we belong.

The happiness that comes with belonging is an elusive and only occasional visitor for most people. Fulfillment and contentment hide out in the shadows or around the corner. (Romans 8:22-24 KJV) *says we, and all creation, are groaning, waiting for the final day of redemption.* This state of longing is indifferent about your country, race or ethnic identity; it doesn't care about your financial status, health, social standing, or your job. Why does everyone have this longing? I believe longing is the human heart calling to God and until God is allowed to fill us, the longing remains. We aren't privy to the design of God. He's the only One who can explain, and the only One who can remove, the longing we experience. *He alone can restore us to the design He planned for us. He wrote all the days of our lives in His book before He placed our substance in our mothers' womb* (Psalm 139:17-18 KJV). He knew us before our human parents knew us. He knew us before we knew ourselves. He designed a plan and purpose for us and our birth was the beginning step toward the fulfillment of that plan. We can wander far from God's plan for our lives. We can reject Him, curse Him, belittle Him, ignore or mock Him. None of that changes His original intention or His plan. Though we have the choice to walk with Him or not, there is no doubt that He's the only One who can restore us to our original design. He's the only one who can remove the longing, reconfigure the broken pieces of our past, and then restore to us everything that has been stolen, lost or broken. Jesus is our only path to reversal and true restoration. In the cross of Christ we find the hero to our story. The Bible says "Believe on the name of the Lord Jesus Christ and You will be saved" (John 5:13 KJV). "Believe in Your heart and confess with Your mouth that Jesus is Lord and you will be saved" (Romans 10:9 KJV). Pretty simple. Believe. He will do the rest if you let Him.

Job is a biblical example of a person suffering through undeserved trials and tragedy. Job was a pillar in his community. Everyone who passed him whispered of his greatness, his prosperity, and his blessings. He was the richest man in the region. People sought him out for advice. He had it all. Everybody wanted to be Job. That is, until his health failed, his livestock died, his children died, the community lost respect for him, his money vanished, and friends no longer sought his counsel.

Those who purported to love him best believed the worst of him. On the day the greatest sorrow befell him he ...said

> Naked came I out of my mother's womb, and naked shall I return: the Lord gave, and the Lord hath taken away; blessed be the name of the Lord. In all this Job sinned not, nor charged God foolishly.
>
> Job 1:21-23 (KJV).

To me this means, Keep trusting in God. Don't falter or fail. God is going to come through for you. He will restore you to your lost estate, whatever it may be. You don't have to go crazy to get back what you lost. God is able.

It may be hard to accept what has happened in your life. It may seem your problems are too big to solve, or your burdens too important to allow God to carry, even that your sins too many to forgive. "With man this is impossible, but with God all things are possible" (Matthew 19:26 KJV). Don't panic, don't give up, and don't give in. God is on His throne and He will help you.

Chapter Four
God is on Your Side

For the Lord God is a Sun and Shield; the Lord bestows [present] glory (honor, splendor and heavenly bliss)! No good thing will He withhold from those who walk uprightly.

__Psalm 84:11 *(AMP)*.

It seems appropriate to review the words we are talking about. What do they really mean? Restore "The act or process of returning something to its original condition by repairing it, cleaning it, etc. The act or process of bringing back to a former position or condition." *The act of returning something stolen or taken, the act of bringing back something that existed before (Emphasis added).* Restitution-"repairing something to an unimpaired or improved condition" (Miriam Webster Dictionary).

These are definitions we can relate to. It says in a few words everything we need to know. It is the act of bringing back something that existed before. How impossible, incredible, and marvelous that sounds. Yet that is exactly what Jesus does for those of us who ask Him to restore us. His eternal aim is to restore us to who we were in the beginning. We will ultimately be who we were before the fall. In this state we will no longer suffer the consequences of being in a fallen world and we will no longer be separated from God.

> And he shall send Jesus Christ, which before was preached unto you, Whom the heavens must receive until the times of restitution of all things, which God hath spoken by the mouth of all his holy prophets since the world began.
>
> Acts 3:21 *(KJV)*

We will no longer be separated from the bright presence of the Father. But we aren't there yet. Our needs are presently defined by negotiating this world, our present circumstance, our often painful past, and our uncertain future. We need restoration for this world and this day. The promise of eternal bliss seems to do little toward solving the problems and circumstances we face right now. God knows that. He understands completely the frailty of our nature, the short span of our lives, and our struggle to find meaning and relevance in it. He never intended to be separated from us and so *He is constantly calling us to return (Zechariah 1:3 KJV). He tells us He will never leave us or forsake us. He won't turn his back on us, He is not a man that He would lie* (Numbers 23:19 KJV). Our part is to return to the Lord. He will do all the rest. He will restore us to what He intended for us since the beginning. No matter your age or situation, there is still time to fulfill your divine destiny and live out the life you were born to have.

When Jesus was on earth and prayed, His prayers were always answered. Scripture tells us why they were answered and how Jesus prayed. If you are looking, longing, and praying for breakthrough, consider how Jesus Himself approached the Father:

1. He went into prayer with a pure heart;
2. He prayed with strong crying and tears;
3. He made specific petitions and requests;
4. He feared being separated from the presence of the Father.

(Hebrews 5:7 AMP)

How much more then, than He, should we pray in this manner? If Jesus went to prayer with specific petitions and requests, we should too. Remember, if Jesus prayed fervently with tears, we dare not be lukewarm in our own petitions and requests. Jesus made certain no guilt, anger, resentment, bitterness, or non-forgiveness stood between Him and the Father. He had a pure heart. There comes a time when we must get serious about our prayers, supplications and entreaties to God. If we expect our prayers to be answered, and if we expect to break through our wall of resistance, we must put ourselves in a most sincere and humble relationship with the Lord "For I am about to do a brand-new thing. See, I have already begun! Do you not see it? I will make a pathway in the wilderness for my people to come home. I will create rivers for them in the desert" (Isaiah 43:19 KJV).

Breakthrough: The dictionary defines Breakthrough "as a sudden, dramatic, and important discovery or development: an instance of achieving success in a particular sphere or activity." *(Oxford on-line Dictionary)* While this brings about an understanding of breakthrough, I believe the dictionary definition is insufficient in explaining what God's Word says about breakthrough. Let's look at "breakthrough" as it was used in the Bible. In King David's second battle, as described in the Old Testament, David was fighting against the Philistines and he defeated them soundly. David named that location and said, "The Lord has broken through my enemies before me like the breaking through of waters" (2 Samuel 5:20 AMP). When one needs breakthrough, call upon the name of the Lord who bursts through like water!

Chapter Five
Foundational Scriptures

There is hope for your future, declares the Lord.
Your children will return to their own territory.
___Jeremiah 31:17 (NIV).

Though I don't usually use the Message Bible as a reference, I do like it. In the case of this first scripture on restoration I find it very compatible with my perception of God's opinion on the subject of restoration. Please use this as just one of the tools in understanding God's plan to restore you or the one for whom you are praying. As always, check many translations of the Bible before you decide what God is saying on any subject.

> Here's what will happen. While you're out among the nations where God has dispersed you and the blessings and curses come in just the way I have set them before you, and you and your children take them seriously and come back to God, your God, and obey him with your whole heart and soul according to everything that I command you today, *God, your God, will restore everything you lost; he'll have* compassion on you; *he'll come back and pick up the pieces* from all the places where you were scattered. No matter how far away you end up, God, *your God, will get you out of there and bring you back* to the land your ancestors once possessed. 1t will be yours again. *He will give you a good life* and make you more numerous than your ancestors. God, your God, will cut away the thick calluses on your heart and your children's hearts, freeing you to love God, your God, with your whole heart and soul and live, really live. God, your God, will put all these curses on your enemies who hated you and were out to get you. And you will make a new start, listening obediently to God, keeping all his commandments that I'm commanding you today. *God, your God, will outdo himself in making things go well for you:* you'll have babies, get calves, grow crops, and enjoy an all-around

good life. Yes, God will start enjoying you again, making things go well for you just as he enjoyed doing it for your ancestors. But only if you listen obediently to God, your God, and keep the commandments and regulations written in this Book of Revelation.

Deuteronomy 30 1-10
(MSG *emphasis added*)

Nothing halfhearted here; you must return to God, your God, totally, heart and soul, holding nothing back.

This commandment that I'm commanding you today isn't too much for you, it's not out of your reach. It's not on a high mountain - you don't have to get mountaineers to climb the peak and bring it down to your level and explain it before you can live it. And it's not across the ocean - you don't have to send sailors out to get it, bring it back, and then explain it before you can live it. No. The word is right here and now - as near as the tongue in your mouth, as near as the heart in your chest. Just do it!

Deuteronomy 30: 1-14 (MSG)

Repent therefore, and turn again, that your sins may be blotted out, that times of refreshing may come from the presence of the Lord, and that he may send the Christ appointed for you, Jesus, whom heaven must receive until the time for restoring all the things about which God spoke by the mouth of his holy prophets long ago.

Acts 3:19-21 (ESV)

I will restore to you the years that the swarming locust has eaten, the hopper, the destroyer, and the cutter, my great army, which I sent among you. You shall eat in plenty and be satisfied, and praise the name of the Lord your God, who has dealt wondrously with you.

Joel 2:25-26 (KJV)

For I will restore health to you, and your wounds I will heal, declares the Lord.

Jeremiah 30:17 (ESV)

The Lord restored the fortunes of Job when he prayed for his friends; and the Lord gave Job twice as much as he had before.

Job 42:10 (AMP)

Chapter Six

Preparing for Strategic Prayer

Jesus answered, 'the most important is, Hear, O Israel: The Lord our God, the Lord is one. And you shall love the Lord your God with all your heart and with all your soul and with all your mind and with all your strength,' the second is this: 'You shall love your neighbor as yourself,' There is no other commandment greater than these.

__Luke 10:27 (CJB)

When embarking on a strategic prayer assignment it's important to evaluate your commitment. Are you willing to stick with it until you receive the desired result? When we agree to pray we are literally taking the life of the person for whom we pray into our hands. Don't leave that person or project unsupported or in danger by abandoning your post.

Important questions to ask before beginning a prayer assignment:

1. Have you fully and freely forgiven those who have offended, betrayed or hurt you? If we carry resentment, bitterness and judgment into our prayer assignments, our prayers will not be heard. "But if you do not forgive others their trespasses, (their reckless and willful sins, leaving them, letting them go, and giving up resentment), neither will your Father in heaven forgive you your trespasses" (Matthew 6:16 AMP).

"Above all things, have intense and unfailing love for one another, for love covers a multitude of sins, forgive and disregard the offenses of others" (1 Peter 4:8 NIV).

2. Do you believe you are fully and freely forgiven by God?

Jesus paid for our redemption in full, once and for all. He did that as a gift to us. We were bought back and restored to our original God-inheritance. His redemption includes being saved from sin, delivered from bondage and healed from disease. Grasp that. The Bible says we are "saved to the uttermost" (Hebrews 7:25 KJV). "When He (Himself and no other) had (by offering Himself on the cross as a sacrifice for sin) accomplished purification from sins and established our freedom from guilt, He sat down (revealing His completed work) at the right hand of the Majesty on high (revealing His Divine authority). For with the heart a person believes in Christ as Savior, resulting in his justification (that is, being made righteous being freed of guilt)" (Hebrews 1:3 AMP). Because of what He did for us, we have the standing to go before His throne to ask for help in our time of need.

3. Do we have the authority to ask for restoration and breakthrough in the name of Jesus?

Yes the scripture clearly gives us that authority. "I have given you power to tread serpents and scorpions underfoot, and to trample on all the power of the enemy; and in no case shall anything do you harm" (Luke 10:19 NIV).

> I assure you and most solemnly say to you, anyone who believes in Me as Savior, will also do the things that I do; and he will do even greater things than these (in extent and outreach) because I am going to the Father. And I will do whatever you ask in My name (as My representative). This I will do so that the Father may be glorified and celebrated in the Son. If you ask Me anything in My name (as My representative) I will do it.
> John 14:12-14 (AMP)

> I will do whatever you ask in My name so that the Father may be glorified through the Son. Yes, I will grant whatever you shall ask in My name (I John 3: 8 KJV). "I assure you most solemnly I tell you, that My Father will grant you whatever you ask in My name."
> John 14:13-14 (AMP)

> Ask and keep on asking and you will receive, so that your joy may be full and complete"

(John 23b and 24b AMP). "Now unto him that is able to do exceeding abundantly above all that we ask or think, according to the power that worketh in us."

Ephesians 3:20 (KJV)

"Blessed [be] the God and Father of our Lord Jesus Christ, who hath blessed us with all spiritual blessings in heavenly [places] in Christ"

(Ephesians 1:3 KJV).

"And the Lord restored the fortunes of Job, when he had prayed for his friends. And the Lord gave Job twice as much as he had before"

(Job 42:10, ESV).

"The Lord hears his people when they cry to Him for help. He rescues them from all their troubles. He is close to the brokenhearted; He rescues those who are crushed in spirit"

(Psalm 34:17 NIV).

"This I know, God is on my side"

(Psalm 56:9b NKJV).

"Surely He has borne our griefs (sicknesses, weaknesses, and distresses). With the stripes that wounded Him we are healed and made whole"

(Isaiah 53 4a-5c AMP).

"With God all things are possible and nothing is impossible"

(Matthew 10:27 NIV).

Now, empowered by His Word and the Holy Spirit, and expecting victory, never worry about anything. Instead, in every situation let your petitions be made known to God through prayers and requests, with thanksgiving.

Philippians 4:6 (AMP)

Chapter Six

Prayers One to Ten

His banner over us is love,
Our sword the Word of God;
We tread the road the saints above
With shouts of triumph trod.
By faith, they like a whirlwind's breath,
Swept on o'er every field.
The faith by which they conquered death
Is still our shining shield. (*John H. Yates 1891*)

Prayer One

Father God, We praise You for Your great love and kindness and we thank You for bringing Doug into our lives. We know You are a God of love and You are waiting and expecting and listening for our prayers so Doug can be restored. We bring our requests and petitions to Your throne just as You taught us.

It is our honor to bring our prayers before You and to ask for help in our time of need. We have assembled a little group of faithful people to pray. This team has committed to pray until we see substantial breakthrough and restoration in Doug's situation. We ask you first, to grant him wisdom and understanding. Teach him to realize only good gifts come from Your hand. We know satan (satan's name doesn't deserve to be capitalized) has been trying to destroy him. We know, according to Your Word, the enemy is a liar, a thief and a destroyer (John 10:10 KJV). However, Yeshua/Jesus came to destroy, demolish and dissolve the works done by the devil (I John 3:8 KJV). We are entreating You to restore all that has been lost, stolen or taken from Doug (Deuteronomy 30:3 KJV). We are asking you to reestablish right relationships between Doug and those who are critical to his well-being. Please repair and restore his career and reputation, return the money and goods stolen from him, and send forth Your Word to heal him. Above all, restore peace and joy to his heart and mind. We pray in the name of Jesus. Amen.

Prayer Two

Father God, You are our Strong Tower, our Protector and our "ever-present, well-timed help in trouble" (Psalms 46:1 AMP).

We cancel the evil assignments causing so much destruction in Doug's life. We cancel every type of witchcraft and sorcery. All curses drawn up to harm him are annulled and canceled. Incantations, evil words and active plots and plans are rendered powerless as are "evil forces in the spiritual realm arrayed against him" (2 Corinthians 10:3-5 KJV). These schemes were rendered powerless when the curse was canceled at the cross of Jesus. Such activity is prohibited. "No weapon raised against Doug will prosper and every evil word spoken against him will be shown to be wrong" (Isaiah 54:17 KJV). "You are a good Father" (James 1:7 KJV), and we ask You to return hope and joy to your child, Doug.

If we lean on and acknowledge You, You will direct our path and grant us the desires of our heart (Proverbs 3:5-6 KJV). Please remember Your Word and hear this prayer.

Send Your mighty angels to surround and protect Doug and to subvert the plans of the enemy. Send your angels to protect him and those he loves. Grant him peace: Give him shalom, with nothing broken, nothing missing and nothing lost. Restore all to him. Thank you for hearing and answering our prayer in the name of Jesus. Amen.

Prayer Three

Father God, All things in heaven and on earth are in subjection to Your Son, Jesus/Yeshua. Through Him we have been given all authority over the power of the enemy (1 Corinthians 15:27 AMP). In His wonderful Name we pray.

Please grant our requests as we pray for Doug's breakthrough and restoration. Thank You for the beautiful children You gave him. Please mend and restore their broken hearts and return them to their father's care. "There is hope for your future, declares the Lord. *Your children will return to their own territory*" (Jeremiah 31:17 NIV emphasis added).

They have heard many lies and curses spoken over their own father and have observed attack after attack against him. This has wounded them badly. Today we declare all ropes, chains and twisted lies will be removed and the pain of separation will be brought to an end. Give Doug and his children eyes to see and ears to hear. Allow them to see clearly the love and need they have for each other. Give them the ability to discern truth from fiction. Envelop them in Your loving arms, and protect them from the wicked one, we pray. Amen.

Prayer Four

Father God, all things in heaven and on earth are in subjection to Your Son, Jesus. You have given Him all authority and, as His children, we share in this authority (Hebrews 2:6-9 NIV). We pray in the name above all Names, Jesus.

Just as You desire us to be in a good relationship with You, we desire Doug to be in a good relationship with his family.

Restore the relationships he longs for. Every boy needs a Dad to love and guide him. Return sons to the arms of their father. Turn the heart of the father to the sons. Restore relationships with daughters. Every daughter longs for a father's love and protection.

Allow those in this broken situation to see good and evil clearly, and to have keen discernment between truth and fiction (1 John 4:1 KJV emphasis added). We cancel now and for all time the strategy the devil has wrought against Doug and his primary relationships. We decree these tactics to be unlawful according to Your Word. *We bind the spirit of fear, and we loose power, love and a sound mind over all involved* (2 Timothy 1:7 KJV emphasis added). Please impart to them the wisdom to see and act in defense of and in favor of what is right and true. We declare all evil plans into which they have been drawn are exposed and immediately ended. Restore all things which concern them.

Father, we request You to dispatch Your mighty angels to protect Doug from "every fiery dart of the wicked one" (Ephesians 6:16 KJV). Allow no harm to be visited upon him in body, mind or spirit. We command the wicked spirits to be silent). We forbid the execution of even one of their evil plans. We bind every retaliatory spirit attempting to take action against any of us who are interceding on behalf of this family.

Send the angelic protection we need to accomplish the task you've laid before us. We praise You for being the Sovereign God of all the universe, but still, our God, who is nearby in times of need. Amen.

Prayer Five

Abba Father, We are so grateful "You are a Mighty and Terrible God. Even Your enemies know this and tremble in Your Presence" (James 2:19 AMP). "We have not come before the Throne of an impotent God made of wood, beads or stone. We come before the Living God, the God of Abraham, Isaac and Jacob" (Matthew 22:32 KJV). "You are the God Who can rend the heavens and come down" (Isaiah 64:1 NIV).

We pray in the name of Jesus, knowing He has *all power and authority on earth and in heaven* (Matthew 28:18 AMP). We know He loves us, bought us with His blood, and has promised good to us. Thank You for hearing us as we pray today.

Make a way for Doug's breakthrough where there is no way. Open the doors before him and lead him to his restoration. Unite him with those he loves. We know "You open doors which cannot be shut" (Isaiah 22:22 KJV). Open the doors of healing for Doug's body, mind and spirit. Open the doors of godly wisdom and understanding. Open the doors of prosperity and plenty. You came that "we might have life and live more abundantly" (John 10:10 KJV). "In the measure we give it will be pressed down, shaken together and overflowing" (Luke 6:38 AMP). "You can do far above what we could even ask or think" (Ephesians 3:20 AMP).

We know Doug constantly thinks about being restored to those he loves. He is aware of all he could do for them and with them. Only You can return lost time and opportunities to him. He is sick at heart and longing for a solution. Answer him with heart peace. Show him the "perfect love that drives out fear: Your perfect love" (1 John 4:18 NIV). We trust beyond a shadow of a doubt that You will reunite and restore Doug to his heart's desire. *You say in "the last days You will turn the hearts of the sons toward their fathers and vice versa* (Luke 1:17 KJV). We proclaim this reunion Let the demons of hell tremble, become confused and fall silent. Our God prevails in all situations and circumstances.

We pray in the mighty name of Jesus. Amen.

Prayer Six

Abba, (Father, in Hebrew) Father, thank You for Your love, kindness, and protection. You have been with us through another year and we are grateful. Only You know what lays ahead so we put our trust in You.

Your word says "You go before us, and hold us by Your mighty right hand. You go beside us and You fence us in. Darkness and light are the same to You" (Psalm 139:5, 10, 11-12 KJV). We are assured of Your help and can do nothing without You. So, we trust You when You say *You will deliver Doug from His troubles* (Psalm 54:7 KJV emphasis added). You have chosen His path and written it in Your book. He has nothing to fear from You or from anything man can do to him. "You are on his side" (Romans 8:31 KJV). You will bring him safely through all that causes him to suffer. You will restore his family to him. You will restore his fortune and return his peace.

You have watched over him throughout his life and you love him. *"You are his righteousness"* (1 Corinthians 1:30 AMP). Impart Doug with the faith of Abraham, faith to wait upon the fulfillment of Your promises; vision like Elijah, to see what's coming; courage like Joseph, to believe in the midst of prison; leadership like David; wisdom like Solomon; strength like Sampson; and love like Jesus. We announce his healing, deliverance, and freedom today. Reverse the damage done to his body, soul and spirit and bring him to the end of affliction. You are the Sovereign of all the universes and all the worlds and have the ability and desire to turn his situation around. "Nothing is too hard for You" (Jeremiah 32:17 AMP). We pray in the name of Jesus, believing. Amen.

Prayer Seven

Father God, Thank You for time. We need time to know You fully, to make amends and right wrongs. We need time to forgive and be forgiven. We need time to find our joy in You. You say "the joy of the Lord is our strength" (Psalm 28:7 AMP). Be our strength we pray.

We "come boldly before Your Throne to ask for help in our time of need" (Hebrews 4:6 KJV). We call upon You in the name of Jesus. Hear us when we pray.

Deliver Doug from the claws of his enemies. Pry off the evil spirits and demonic forces that have been working to destroy him and his relationships Break through to touch hardened hearts, restore his health and return his prosperity, we pray. Evil forces are working to destroy his good name, steal all his worldly goods and dissolve his family. We say "no!" Stand up for his help, Lord! You tell us we can "bind on earth what is bound in heaven and loose on earth what is loosed in heaven" (Matthew 16:19 KJV). To this end we bind all these demons of hell who are pursuing him for the sake of doing evil against him. We literally command them back to their hiding place and forbid them to return or send any replacements. This is the first day of freedom from this relentless onslaught.

We bind lying tongues. We bind slander and gossip regarding Doug and his situation. No evil words are allowed to curse him or turn those he loves away from him.

> We are not fighting against flesh-and-blood enemies, but against evil rulers and authorities of the unseen world, against mighty powers in this dark world, and against evil spirits in the heavenly places. (Ephesians 6:12 NLT)

We have the authority, and we take that authority, to pull down the stronghold of hate and vengeance built up against Doug. We proclaim him to be a righteous man of valor and integrity. Take his side, O Lord, in this raging battle. Help him. "Silence and forestall the enemies contending against him" Psalms 3:7 (KJV).

You are a mighty and powerful God. "All things are possible with You and nothing is impossible" (Mark 9:23 KJV). Thank you for inclining Your ear to our prayer and running to our help. Amen.

Prayer Eight

Father God, In the name of Jesus we enter Your Throne Room. We are grateful You are a powerful God. You are exalted on high and can see our entire life from beginning to end. "You rescue Your children day after day and look after those who are called by Your name" (2 Timothy 4:18 NIV).

"You build up kings and kingdoms, and tear them down whenever You want" (Jeremiah 1:10 KJV). You are not constrained by the laws of man nor the laws of nature or physics. It's so amazing.

We pray with Your eternal attributes in our mind. We believe the evidence tells us You will restore our friend completely if we keep asking. We ask in agreement with Your Word and pray: "May the Spirit of the Lord rest on [Doug], the Spirit of wisdom, and understanding, the spirit of council and might, the spirit of knowledge and the spirit of reverential fear" (Isaiah 2:11 AMP).

We are not speaking as the world speaks and understands, but as You speak. Give Doug the strategies and tactics to safely navigate the terrain unfolding before him. Open his eyes and ears so he will hear You as You guide, act, and speak the truth required for his complete deliverance. Restore him to his loved ones, his health, his joy, and his fortune. "We know Your ways are above our ways" (Isaiah 55:9 KJV). In fact, You say "the wisdom of the world is foolishness to You" (1 Corinthians 3:19 AMP). Give Doug Your wisdom, the wisdom of Solomon, the wisdom of Jesus, so he won't falter anywhere along the way. *Now is the day of salvation and deliverance* (2 Corinthians 6:2 KJV). Now, today, is the day of restoration and breakthrough.

Thank you for hearing and answering our prayer. Amen.

Prayer Nine

In the mighty name of Jesus we pray. We have permission to approach because we are robed in the righteousness of Christ. With praise and thanksgiving, being anxious for nothing, we bring our prayers for Doug's restoration to You (Philippians 4:6 NKJV).

We expect and believe You will intervene in Doug's life and change his situation. Please burst through the obstacles he faces and deliver him. We know You will not rest until his life is restored completely.

We ask You to keep his alienated relationships in mind. These are so hurtful. Do your wonderful work in the hearts and minds of those who stand aloof from him for no reason. Break through the confusion and conflicted loyalties and expose the truth. Lead them in integrity to healing and freedom.

We declare those broken and missing things in Doug's life are restored to him (James 4:7 AMP). We release the joy of the Lord to be Doug's strength during this battle. We agree with Your Word and declare:

This is what the Lord Your Creator says:

> He, who formed you, 'Do not fear, for I have redeemed you. I have called you by name. You are mine! When you pass through the waters, I will be with you, and through rivers, they will not overwhelm you, when you walk through fire, you will not be scorched, nor will the flame burn you, for I am the Lord Your God, the Holy One of Israel, your Savior. Because you are precious in My sight, you are honored and I love you.'
>
> Isaiah 43:2 (KJV)

Carry Doug to a place of safety we pray. Thank You for hearing our prayer. You are worthy of all glory and honor. Amen.

Prayer Ten

Abba, Thank You for another day of life. Thank you for a world full of beautiful mountains and valleys and oceans and trees. Thank you for all You have given us: a place to live and sleep; food to eat; and friends and companions. We are so grateful for all these wonderful gifts and recognize how generous You are to us. Thank You for this assignment to pray for Doug's restoration.

Today we declare breakthrough for him. *We declare wisdom and a discerning spirit. He needs to see only the truth in the matter before him* (1 Thessalonians 5:21 AMP). We declare all evil plots, collaborations, plans and snares will be exposed. We expect recompense and reward to accumulate for him. We proclaim:

> Wisdom resides with prudence and good judgment, moral courage and common sense. It finds knowledge and discretion and includes hatred of evil, pride, arrogance and the evil way, and it (wisdom) hates the perverted mouth. It walks in the righteous way amidst the paths of justice. It will bring riches and honor and enduring wealth to those who have it.
> Proverbs 8:12-37 (KJV)

As Doug grows in Your wisdom, we trust in You and the bond of Your Word. Our expectation is in You, O Lord. *We therefore go into the enemy's camp and take back EVERYTHING that has been stolen (Joel 2:25 NIV emphasis added)*. We declare Doug is blessed and not cursed. He is blessed because he listens to You and heeds Your Word. Every curse from any source is broken in the powerful name of Jesus. He walks with wisdom, insight and understanding. His days and years will be multiplied. Evil plans are overturned and exposed. He obtains favor and grace from the Lord. We declare he and his household are blessed going out and coming in. They are at peace, prosperous and at rest. *Everything he puts his hand to will prosper* (2 Corinthians 9:8 NIV).

We declare his enemies are defeated and brought to justice. All will be restored (Job 42:7-17 KJV).

We pray in the name and authority of Jesus. Please hear our prayers and decrees. Amen.

Chapter Seven

Prayers Eleven through Twenty-One

Oh, Lord, give me back my joy again, You have broken me-now let me rejoice.

Renew a right spirit within me. Do not banish me from Your presence, and don't take Your Holy Spirit from me. Restore me to the joy of Your salvation.

The sacrifice You desire is a broken spirit. O God, You will not reject a broken and contrite heart.

__Psalm 51: 8-11, 16-17 *(NLT)*

Prayer Eleven

Abba, "Behold You desire truth in the innermost being, and in the hidden part You will make me know wisdom" (Psalm 51: 6 NLT). "Teach me Your way, O Lord; I will walk in Your truth. Unite my heart to fear Your name" (Psalm 86:11 NLT).

Today we ask for Your famous mercy, justice, and loving kindness (Proverbs 21:3 KJV), as we pray for reversal and restoration for our friend Doug. Lord, You know the motivation of his heart and the thoughts in his head. You know every good deed and sacrifice he has made on behalf of others. You know his acts of heroism and of his kindnesses done in secret. You have forgiven his faults and shortcomings, and led him along a pathway of integrity.

We know You are aware that complaints, accusations, and illegal decrees have been unjustly charged to Doug's account. Lies have been told, property and possessions have been confiscated. His children have been used as weapons in a battle which is not theirs. His primary relationships have been gravely affected and compromised. Those needing Doug's love and protection are forcibly separated from it.

Lord, arise and scatter his enemies (Psalm 68:1 KJV). "Put on Your shield and buckler and come to his defense. Let those who hate him flee before him. Let the wicked and guilty be exposed with their plots and plans. Show Yourself strong and act on his behalf. Answer him according to the greatness of Your compassion, turn to him" (Psalm 69:16-18 KJV). *Ransom him from his enemies who delight in his distress and we will give you the honor and glory as you deserve* (Psalm 55:18-23 NIV). Revive and renew him, comfort and restore him. Our requests are made in the name of Jesus. Thank You for hearing and answering our prayers. Amen.

Prayer Twelve

Abba Father, We rejoice in this day You have made. We are glad and have hope for Doug's breakthrough today. There is no circumstance or situation too hard for you to handle. You build Kings and Kingdoms, then tear them down (Daniel 2:20-21 KJV). You have delegated all power and authority in every realm to Your Son, Jesus the Messiah, in whose name we pray (Matthew 28:18 KJV).

Yes, Doug has sufferings, trials, difficult situations, troubles; but You deliver the righteous from them all (Psalms 34:19 KJV). Today we can say:

The Lord God is *Doug's* strength, *his* source of courage, *his* invincible army; He has made *Doug's* feet steady and sure like hind's feet and makes *him* walk forward with spiritual confidence on *his* high places of challenge and responsibility.
Habakkuk 3:19 (AMP) Italic's added)

Today, Doug will be strong and very courageous (Deuteronomy 31:6 KJV). He puts his trust and faith in You to act on his behalf and vindicate him. He will hear Your still small voice guiding him. Today lies will be exposed and wrongs will be put right. Today will be a day of blessing and favor. Our hope and confidence are in You. "You will never, no never, forsake us" (Hebrews 13:5 KJV). You are the God of renewal and restoration. "Righteousness and justice are the foundation of Your Throne" (Psalms 89:14 KJV). *Answer us when we call, God of righteousness; we know you will free Doug now when he is hemmed in, and relieve him in his distress; be gracious to him and hear and respond to our prayers* (2 Corinthians 4:8 KJV). We thank You. Amen.

Prayer Thirteen

Abba, Thank You for Your gracious goodness to us. Thank You for providing clear instructions so we can seek, know and follow after You. You are more than enough for the children of men.

Forgive us for putting anything ahead of You. We remember Your Word which says, "Our power is not carnal, but mighty before God for the pulling down of strongholds" (2 Corinthians 10:4 AMP). Thank You for this transfer of power. You say where "sin abounds, grace abounds more" (Romans 5:20 AMP).

In the name of Jesus we exercise our power and pull down the stronghold of deceit, fabrication, fanciful tales, robbery and cover-up that has built up this stronghold against Doug. We know "You are not a man that You should lie" (Numbers 23:19 KJV). If You break Your Word the universe stops in its very tracks. We are putting all our hope and trust in You and Your Word. We know You are looking and longing to restore Doug because You are the God of Restoration.

You will make Doug whole, as it is You who fills all things everywhere with Your Presence (Exodus 33:14 KJV). He will be vindicated and receive double recompense for every wrong. His family will be restored to him. As John Newton said in "Amazing Grace," "The Lord has promised good to us, His Word, our hope secures; He will our Shield and Portion be, as long as life endures." Surround Doug with Your favor like a shield and let Him see Your goodness now, in the land of the living. "May Thy kingdom come and Thy will be done" (Matthew 6:10 KJV). Amen.

Prayer Fourteen

Bend the heavens and come down to minister to Doug today. Shift the entire universe if You must and hear our cry for His help. Reach out Your mighty right hand to hold him and guide him on his way. Be his rear guard and protect him from all evil (Psalms 144:5-7 NIV).

Work in his body, soul, and spirit to restore his joy, his peace, and his hope. Make changes on his behalf. Lift the despair and despondency he's been experiencing and give him a heart of gratitude. *We declare today, Doug will never again be put to shame for You will deliver and rescue him* (Romans 10:11 AMP). *You have inclined Your ear and You will save him. You are his shelter and he can come to You anytime. You are his rock and fortress. Rescue him from the grasp of the wicked and ruthless who have conspired against him. Vindicate him* (Psalms 54:1-7 NIV). You never abandon us, especially when our own strength is used up and gone. Cut off those who pursue him. Stay near to him and let his enemies be exposed along with all their trickery and schemes.

Protect and shelter him and his family. *Cast Your shadow over them and make them invisible to the evil one. Send Your angels to provide protection so their hearts will not be damaged or afraid* (Psalms 91: 1:11 KJV). Give them a sense of certainty regarding Your love. Don't allow them to be misled. You are the Mighty God with whom all things are possible. We love and worship You alone. In the name of Jesus we pray. Amen.

Prayer Fifteen

Almighty God, our Creator and Sovereign, Thank You for teaching us Your ways. We know people perish for lack of knowledge (Hosea 4:6 AMP), so make us wise. Thank You for placing Your Spirit, the spirit of knowledge, within us.

Lead us in the way ever-lasting, make us students of Your Wisdom and seekers of Your Truth. Thank You for the Holy Spirit and Your infinite love towards us. Thank You for canceling the claims placed upon us by the evil one and for purchasing our redemption through Jesus.

You have given us the keys to Your Kingdom (Matthew 16:19 AMP), *and given us the faith we need to move mountains into the sea* (Mark 11:23 KJV) and to declare a thing and see it be so. Today we bind and forbid the evil one in his efforts to destroy Doug. We forbid any evil directed against him. We forbid false statements and accusations and we declare that the truth will be known to all involved. We stand on the side of integrity and reason. We loose (permit) stolen property in all forms to be restored to Doug. We proclaim his family will be restored to him. We loose the joy of his salvation, the hope of his childhood, the strength and courage of a lion, the expectation of Your goodness and *the heart peace that surpasses all understanding* (Philippians 4:7 KJV). We put our hope and expectation in You. In the name of Jesus, hear our prayer. Amen.

Prayer Sixteen

Abba Father,

You are our Rock. Your work is perfect, for all Your ways are law and justice. You are a God of faithfulness, without breach or deviation. You are right and just. We beseech You to open wide Your hands and give {Doug} help against his adversaries, for vain is the help of man.

Psalms 31:3 (NIV)

"You are the great and all knowing God" *(1 John 5:20 NIV)*.

Arise, O Lord, and confront and forestall Doug's enemies and give him the hidden treasures they have stolen. Loose the bonds of wickedness, undo the bonds of oppression and set him free from the prison of despair and hopelessness.
Psalms 142:7 (AMP; Doug added)

Restore him. Break every yoke constraining him. Guide him continually through these dry places and make his bones strong so he will be able to stand his ground whatever the circumstance (Isaiah 58:11 KJV).

Give him boundless might, strength and support. Restore his fortunes and the fortunes of his forefathers. Do him good only. Prosper every work of his hands and bring him to victory. Revive him in the midst of his troubles. "Forsake not the work of Your own hands" *(Psalms 90:17 KJV)*.

We give You all praise, glory and honor in the name of Jesus. Amen.

Prayer Seventeen

In the mighty name of Jesus we pray. Today we bring Doug's family to you, wherever they may be scattered. They are growing up so fast. Please reach out Your mighty hand and calm their worries and anxieties. They are suffering more than they themselves even realize. This is a mess only You can put right.

You say You "hate an unbalanced scale and those who rush to do evil" (Proverbs 11:1 KJV). Deliver Doug's children to the protection of those who truly love them, we pray. You speak of Your wisdom. You say Your Wisdom is understanding, power and strength.

Riches and honor are with You, enduring wealth and right standing with God. Wisdom walks in the righteous way, in the midst of the paths of justice, and causes those who love wisdom to inherit true wealth and riches (Proverbs 8:14, 18, 20, 21 AMP).

We seek Your Wisdom, Lord, as we pray for Doug and ask You to bestow Your wisdom upon him. Open his ears and eyes to Your truth so his decisions and actions will be filled with right standing and justice. Honor him with restoration and restitution. Bring him deliverance from this thorny situation. Illuminate his thinking with Your light. Protect and guard his heart. Protect him from the evil one. Bring him peace in the midst of the storm and calm his fears. *When the enemy comes in like a flood, raise a banner of love over him* (Song of Solomon 2:4 KJV). Thank You for hearing and answering our prayers through the mighty name of Jesus, Amen.

Prayer Eighteen

Father, Thank You for being the same, yesterday, today and forever. There is no shadow of turning with You. You are one hundred percent faithful, reliable and dependable (Hebrews 13:8 KJV).

We can stand on Your promises without fear of shame or disappointment. You are filled with loving-kindness and readily forgive us when we repent with our whole heart. Our shortcomings and guilt are hidden from Your eyes. How great is that?

Thank You for hearing our cries day after day; for inclining Your ear to Doug's dilemma, *for having a plan to do good to him, for already working in his future to bring Your plan to fruition* (Jeremiah 29:11 KJV).

We present Doug's family to You. *Release their angels to guard them* (Luke 4:10 KJV). You say "the power of life and death is in the tongue" (Proverbs 18:21 AMP), so today we proclaim his family will choose life, they will pursue and find the destiny You have for them. Impart Your peace, joy, and love into each heart.

Essential elements of the family foundation have been relentlessly chipped away by words of anger, defeat, and discouragement. The family has been separated from You and from one another. This is devastating, Lord, and Doug is suffering terribly. We pray such words will not be spoken again. Please replace them with words of love and encouragement.

We release mercy and grace to restore them, kindness and patience to rebuild them and hope and faith to return them to being a family once and for all. *Protect their hearts, for out of the heart flows the river of life* (John 7: 38 KJV). Fill their hearts with good things. Bring Your justice to them. Turn their hearts toward You and bring them to a place of peace. Give Doug wisdom and understanding as You deliver him and his family from the snare the enemy has used to entangle them. Thank you for hearing our prayer in the name of Jesus. Amen.

Prayer Nineteen

Abba Father, We acknowledge You as The Alpha and Omega, the I Am, the true and living God of Abraham, Isaac and Jacob. "You are our Shield and Defender, our Fortress and High Tower" (Psalms 18:2 AMP). All that we have comes from Your hand (1 Chronicles 29:16 AMP). Your Great Name goes with us in darkness and light alike.

Restore Doug with Your peace: that peace which passes all understanding. Reveal Your love for him. *Help him set aside all guilt so You can hear his prayer* (Psalms 86:6 AMP). He doesn't need to worry about vengeance or making even the score as You will take care of that. *He can stand still and watch Your deliverance* (Psalms 46:10 KJV). Cause his mind to rest so You can renew it with good things. Let him review Your generosity and kindness to him throughout the years of his life as he regards his own sacrificial acts of duty and heroism. *Remove all his fears as he puts his trust in You and not in man* (Exodus 14:13-14 KJV). You, O Lord, are a Father. You understand perfectly the pain in his heart. You identify with his suffering. You know how he longs for a restored relationship with his family. Grant this to him we pray.

We acknowledge You in all our ways; please grant us our heart's desire (Proverbs 3:5-6 KJV). We pray in the name of Your own Son, Jesus the Messiah. Amen.

Prayer Twenty

Oh Lord, We will declare and publish Your goodness and praise You from generation to generation. Restore us O God of Hosts. Cause Your face to shine upon us and we will be saved. Bestow on us grace, favor and honor (Psalm 80:1-7 AMP). "No good thing will You withhold from him who walks uprightly" (Psalms 84:11 KJV).

Please grant Doug peace in place of strife and disruption. He is very important to You, we know. You have planned good for him. You Have heard of his courage, you know his strengths and weaknesses. He longs for Your help. *Protect his life and save him from distress* (Psalms 32:7 KJV). *Teach him Your ways and grant him Your strength, might and power. Let those who hate him be ashamed* (Psalms 86:17 KJV).

> You have a strong arm. Mighty is Your hand. Truth goes before You. Vindicate and restore him. No longer allow the wicked to humiliate or outwit him. Crush his adversaries. Do not allow Your faithfulness to fail.
>
> Psalms 89:23 NLT; him added

Give him a teachable spirit, a humble heart and a keen mind.

> May he grow in grace and thrive, bear fruit and prosper in his old age. Allow him to flourish and be vital and fresh, rich in trust, love and contentment. Let him be a living memorial to the faithfulness of Your promises.
>
> Psalms 92:13-15 (AMP)

Guard and protect him and his children and keep them far from the evil one. Keep their angels at high alert so misfortune will not find them. Restore them all, in the name of Jesus. Amen.

Prayer Twenty-One

Our God and Father, Your Word is living and powerful, and sharper than any two edged sword, piercing even to the dividing asunder of soul and spirit, and of the joints and marrow, and is a discerner of the thoughts and intents of the heart.
Hebrews 4:12 (KJV)

Thank You for Your Living Word, and for Jesus Christ, who gave His blood as a Covenant to us. He has purchased and redeemed us.

"In Him is life and power and the light of life. This light shines on in darkness and darkness cannot understand, overpower or absorb it. This light enlightened everyone and continues to shine" (John 1:4-5 NLT). We thank You for the light and for Your enduring truth. Our steadfast hope is in You alone.

We appropriate Your promises for Doug today. Your grace, and not our works, has activated these promises in Doug's life. Give him the childlike hope and faith he needs to trust You. *You have promised good to him and plan to work what the devil means for bad together for good on his behalf. Through You he will do valiantly* (Genesis 50:20 KJV).

His family is in an emergency situation and Your wisdom and understanding are necessary to come up with a good solution. Please dispatch extra angels to protect them as You work to remove all the obstacles they face. Give Doug a steadfast heart that trusts in You alone.

We cast all our cares on You. In the name of Jesus, Amen.

Chapter Eight

Prayers Twenty-Two to Thirty-Two

You will pull me out of the net which they have secretly laid for me, for You are my strength. You hide them (your people) in the secret place of Your presence from the conspiracies of man; You keep them secretly in a shelter from the strife of tongues. Blessed be the Lord for He has made marvelous His loving-kindness to me in a besieged city.

___Psalm 31: 3, 20, 24 (AMP)

Prayer Twenty-Two

Lord, in the name of Jesus we pray. We enter Your gates with thanksgiving and Your courts with praise. We know You incline Your ear to persistent and insistent prayer and You answer us because we believe You will keep Your promises. We thank You.

Father, there is a conspiracy and collaboration drawn up against Doug. We come against these diabolical plans and cancel them. We are looking to Your great mercy and believing in complete restoration. *We loose truth and demand the enemy release restitution and repayment of what has been stolen* (Jeremiah 30:17 KJV). Give Doug all the strength and stamina he needs to persist in his efforts to restore his family. Don't let his enemies waste his time or energy on anything which will further erode his resources and bring no good result. Instead, *Prosper and bless all his work* (Psalms 90:17 KJV). You will deliver him from all his enemies. Amen.

Prayer Twenty-Three

Almighty God, maker of heaven and earth, thank You for considering us and hearing us when we pray. Let all creation sing Your praises.

We have cried out for Your help day and night. Let our prayers for Doug come before You and enter Your presence. Incline Your ear to his complicated situation. Your enduring Light overcomes darkness. Shine Your light into the deepest darkness. Expose the secrets and plans the adversary has raised against him. Have mercy on him and hear him. Strengthen him and sustain him with Your mighty, outstretched right arm. *Teach him to number his days; give him a heart of wisdom. Satisfy him now, before he grows older so he can rejoice and be glad all his days. Confirm the work of his hands and shine Your favor upon him* (Psalm 90:14-16 AMP).

We loose, according to Your Word, immediate restitution and repayment for all things illegally taken from him. We prohibit any new plans being made or executed by his enemies. We forbid the wrongful seizure of any of his assets and we demand the return of those unjustly taken from him. You say: "the righteous will flourish like a date palm, long-lived, upright and useful; growing in grace they will bear fruit and prosper in old age. They are living memorials to declare the Lord is a promise keeper" (Psalm 92:12-15 AMP). We bind these words to his heart as we agree together that these promises are true for him.

Permit him to be restored to the heart of his family. Let them look on him as a hero, a loving father and a trustworthy man of his word. Turn their thought toward him for his good. Cause them to recognize and believe the truth regarding his loyalty and faithfulness to them. Keep his family safe from the evil one. We pray in the name of Jesus. Amen.

Prayer Twenty Four

*Our loving Father, Great is Your name and worthy
to be praised. You fill all things everywhere with
Your Presence (Ephesians 4:6 KJV). Thank You,
Our praise and prayers are always before You
(Psalm 141:2 KJV). Thank You for the blood of
Jesus which covers our transgressions and makes
it possible for us to speak directly to You.*

Grant justice to Doug. Remember all the times he chose to serve You and his fellow man, as well as to do the right thing. Remember his integrity. "Let the wickedness of the wicked come to an end" (Psalm 7:9 KJV). Maintain his cause by cutting off his enemy. You do not abandon those who seek you. You are his shield and defense. We release health, favor and blessing over Doug. We demand the enemy completely restore all he has taken.

"You are our refuge and stronghold in times of trouble" (Psalm 9:9 KJV). We put our confident trust in You. Restore Doug and execute justice on his behalf. Amen.

Prayer Twenty-Five

Father God, Thank You for Your many blessings toward us. Thank You for grace and mercy, for strength for the day, for mercies that are new each morning. "But I will sing of Your strength, In the morning I will sing of Your love; for You are our fortress, our refuge in times of trouble" (Psalm 59:16 NIV). Thank You for being our rear guard (Isaiah 58:8 KJV), and for keeping us away from danger and evil. Thank You for caring about us and for listening when we pray. Help us show You how grateful we are.

We remind You about Your son, Doug. He is still in need of our prayers and faith. He is still in need of Your deliverance. He has been dragged into a snare. We ask You to extricate him without further harm, to bring him out to a large place, to set his feet on solid ground. Act on his behalf so he will know beyond every doubt how much You care for him. Show him how You have guided his steps and illuminated his path all this while. Show him how You have called his name since the very beginning of his life. Bring him into a right relationship with You. Speak to the very center of his bones so he will know it is You. Give him Your peace and joy. Restore him in every sense and return with interest all he has lost.

Prepare him for all his upcoming battles. *Clothe him with Your wisdom and understanding* (Isaiah 11:2 AMP). Expose the strategy and tactics employed by his opponents so all secrets and lies will be laid bare. You have a heart for Doug's plight, so grant restitution and reunion for him and his family. Open the hidden vaults and reveal and return his stolen treasures. "You hate injustice and an unbalanced scale is an offense to You"

(Proverbs 11:1 KJV). We entreat You to balance the scale and bring him justice.

"You, O Lord, are a shield for us, our glory, and the lifter of our head" (Psalm 3:3 KJV). Jesus, Thank You for hearing and answering prayer. Amen.

Prayer Twenty-Six

Abba, We bless You O Lord, You forgive our sins
and heal all our diseases. You have redeemed us
from the pit and crowned us with lavish kindness
and mercy. You execute righteousness for the
oppressed. You are merciful and gracious, slow
to anger and abounding in compassion.

Psalm 103:3, 4, 8 (NIV)

Just as Doug loves his children, so You love us, who are filled with awe of You. May Your glory endure forever.

Thank You for looking sympathetically upon Doug's distress. Remember Your promises towards him. As we cry to You concerning his trouble, rescue him and allow him to establish his home. *You do wonderful acts for the children of men* (Psalm 65:5 KJV). You are no respecter of persons.

Bring Doug out of his financial and personal bondage and set him on high, away from affliction and disease. *We bind the mouths of the wicked and deceitful. No more is he a victim of a lying tongue. We forbid the harsh accusations of those who have surrounded him with words of hatred and, in return for love, have attacked him* (Psalm 109:2-4 KJV). We release good for him and forbid wickedness to prosper against him. We call for the release of financial freedom and prosperity.

Protect him and his family and keep them from the evil one. You alone can change a heart and re-kindle understanding. Thank You for hearing our prayers which are presented in the name of Jesus. Amen.

Prayer Twenty-Seven

Abba, what an amazing and never to be underestimated Father You are! Your thoughts toward us are more than the sands of the sea. You plan for our good and not our harm (Jeremiah 29:11 KJV).

Have you not known? Have you not heard? The everlasting God, the Lord, the Creator of the ends of the earth, does not faint or grow weary; there is no searching of his understanding. He gives power to the faint and weary and to him who has no might he increases strength and causes it to multiply and abound.

Isaiah 40: 28-29 (AMP)

We release increased strength and endurance to Doug. *He is strong in the power of Your might* (Ephesians 6:10 KJV). He knows You are his help and his salvation. You will guide him and even carry him when necessary. You will not allow him to be overcome. We release justice, restoration and a wonderful reunion on his behalf. Surround him with those who speak and live truth.

You say: we are defined by the fruit of our mouth; and with the consequence of words we must be satisfied, whether good or evil. Death and life are in the power of the tongue and they who indulge in it shall eat the fruit of it. (Proverbs 18:29-21 AMP)

Please take notice and expose deadly and lying words directed toward Doug. Release continual angelic and Godly protection for him.

We pray in the name of Jesus as we release Your peace and joy to Your son Doug. Amen.

Prayer Twenty-Eight

Abba, Father, You are the God who rides through the heavens to our help (Deuteronomy 33:26 KJV). It is Your great name that puts kings in place and builds kingdoms (Daniel 2:21 KJV). The gold and silver are Yours; the earth and everything in it (Haggai 2:8 KJV). It is You who numbers the hairs of our head and writes the days of our life in Your book (Psalm 139:16 AMP). How could we but put our trust and hope in You?

Give Doug wisdom. Vindicate him with the power of Your mighty right hand. Deliver him out of the snares and traps set for him. Surround him with a throng of angels who work on his behalf to protect, reveal and uncover. Give him the humble heart he needs to meet his family in their own brokenness and begin the healing process among them. Fill him with the life of Your love, bind bitterness and restrain it from taking root in his life. We release truth and only truth over him. Thank You for always guarding us. Keep him, his family, and all of us from the evil one. In the name of Jesus we pray. Amen.

Prayer Twenty-Nine

We love You fervently and devotedly, O Lord our Strength. You are our Rock, our Fortress, and our Deliverer; our God, our keen and firm Strength in whom we trust and take refuge' our Shield, and the horn of our salvation, our High Tower. We call upon the Lord, Who is to be praised, so shall we be saved from our enemies.

Psalms 18:1-2 (NIV)

We thank You Lord, for all You are to us, and we praise You for delivering Doug from the hands of his enemies. We are truly confident You are acting on His behalf right now. *You lift him up above those who rise up against him* (Psalm 18:48 KJV). We exalt You. Thank You. Your Word revives Doug and gives him hope.

"Lord, You are the God of all flesh. There isn't anything too hard for You" (Jeremiah 32:27 KJV). You can restore even the most shattered lives and mend the impossibly broken heart. You are the author of right relationships and "You keep Covenant to the thousandth generation" (Deuteronomy 7:9 KJV). There is nothing in Doug's life You can't fix. We loose hope and faith over Doug. Illuminate his heart, restore and heal him. Reveal Yourself to him and his household. *Chip all the stone away from our hearts that they will be soft and pliable before You* (Ezekiel 36:26 KJV). Protect his children and family; restore him to his rightful place in their lives.

Forgive us of our failures and shortcomings and keep the evil one far from us. In the name of Jesus we pray. Amen.

Prayer Thirty

Abba Father, We thank You that You "will not break a bruised reed, nor quench a dimly burning flame. No, You bring it forth in justice and in truth. You will not fail until You establish justice in the earth" (Isaiah 42:3-4 KJV)!

Thank *You for Your Word which is alive and full of power* (Hebrews 4:12 NIV). You will establish justice for Doug! You will restore him. What incredible promises these are!

Father, thank You, for hearing our prayers. We are fully expecting great things. We know "You will do all Your pleasure and purpose and Your counsel will stand" (Isaiah 46:10 KJV). *You will vindicate him before all who have raised weapons against him and no weapon will find its mark* (Isaiah 54:17 KJV).

Reveal Yourself as the Lord of love and mercy. We tear down the stronghold of fear over him and his family. You have given us this mighty power and we employ it to break the bonds of negativity, untruth, and falsehoods that are imprisoning the family. Their life is before them. Teach them to rejoice and be glad. Free them from this fight. Assure them all will be well. Show them the purity of Doug's love toward them. Gently enable them to perceive and understand the truth. Help them guard their hearts against destructive attacks. We fit the armor of God to Doug; *the helmet of salvation, the breastplate of righteousness, the belt of truth, the shield of faith and the sandals of the good news of the gospel. Help us teach him to use the sword of the Spirit (which is the word of God) to defend against all the wiles of the devil* (Ephesians 6:11-18 KJV).

The wickedness of this age is on the rise. The devil has gained a foothold. Give Doug the tools he needs to reverse the destruction done to his family and to him. They have a strong foundation. Build on that. Give them time together, heart to heart talks, respect for one another, increased understanding, and lots of love. We thank You for being a Father who cares about everything which concerns us. *Thank You for leaving us Your peace. Our hearts are not troubled or afraid* (John 14:27 AMP).

> We won't be agitated or disturbed or distressed and we won't be fearful, intimidated or cowardly. We put all our hope and trust in You because we know You are on our side, therefore, no foe can bring us to ruin.
>
> Psalm 34:18-19 *(NIV)*

In the name of Jesus, the Name above all names, we pray. Amen.

Prayer Thirty-One

Father God, We fling ourselves on You in absolute confidence that you hear us when we pray. We gratefully acknowledge that You listen to what we ask of You and we have assured certainty that You have already granted us our requests (1 John 5:14-15, 18 AMP).

Thank You for not leaving us as orphans, and for sending us the Holy Spirit, to comfort us and to lead us into all truth. *We know we have no power or might on our own but the Spirit can accomplish all things* (John 14: 18, 19, 26 AMP). Continue to pour out the Wisdom of God on Doug and give him the understanding to grasp and apply it.

Lord, Jesus, bring judges to Doug's court proceedings that care about the restoration of this family. We ask for judicial discernment and partiality to the truth.

> We know the corruption among judges is rampant. It's causing the foundations of the earth to be shaken. They judge unjustly and show partiality to the wicked. They walk in darkness and show no understanding. O Judge of all nations, bring justice for (Doug).
> Psalms 82:2, 5, 8 (KJV; Doug added)

We release every good thing over Doug: restoration, health, recompense, rejuvenation, wisdom, understanding, confidence in You, mental clarity, and a calm spirit. Grant him "The fruits of the Spirit: love, joy, peace, forbearance, kindness, goodness faithfulness, gentleness and self control. Against such things there is no law" (Galatians 5: 22-23 AMP).

We bind wickedness and vengeance. We forbid proceedings with false claims and slanderous accusations. We release truth and exposure of the facts. We ask that Doug's enemies will be stricken with remorse and repentance. We pray they will be shocked at their own depravity and will turn from their evil ways. We forbid greed and the love of money from ruling Doug's situation.

We bind every crafty scheme. Garrison Doug's heart with Your love and surround him with peace.

"Let the redeemed of the Lord say so, those whom he has delivered from the hand of his adversary" (Psalm 107:2 KJV). Hear our prayers in the name of Jesus. Amen.

Prayer Thirty-Two

Abba Father, "Who is God, but the Lord? Or who is a rock, except our God, the God who encircles us with strength and makes our way blameless? He makes our feet like hinds' feet (able to stand firmly and tread safely on paths of testing and trouble); He sets us securely upon high places. He enlarges the path beneath us and makes our steps secure so our feet won't slip. We have been trained to fight and can bend a bow of bronze."

Psalms 18:31-34 (AMP)

"You are great O Lord and greatly to be praised" *(Psalm 48:1 KJV)*.

Thank You for being on Doug's side. *He cannot be swallowed alive, the waters cannot engulf him, he cannot be ripped apart by those lying in wait for him. The trap is broken and Doug has escaped because his help is in the Lord, the Maker of heaven and earth* (Psalm 41:1-4 AMP).

Lord, You say children are a heritage and gift from You. Children need their father, just as we need You. Call Doug's children to him. We request that a longing need for him be placed in their hearts. We release courage to enable them to step forward and declare their love for their father. Remove them from situations that are painful and damaging. Release peace of heart and mind over them. We put You in remembrance of Your Word and ask for justice.

We give You thanks with all our heart and have confidence You will accomplish all that concerns Doug. In the name of Jesus, hear our prayer and save us from the evil one. Amen.

Chapter Ten

Prayers Thirty-Four to Forty-Four

The tongue is a small thing that makes grand speeches. But a tiny spark can set a great forest on fire. And among all the parts of the body, the tongue is a flame of fire. It is a whole world of wickedness, corrupting your entire body. It can set your whole life on fire, for it is set on fire by hell itself.

___James 3:3-6 *(NLT)*

Prayer Thirty-Four

Abba, Thank You for hearing us when we pray.
"May Your glorious name be blessed and exalted
above all blessing and praise. You are the Lord,
You alone; You have made the heavens, the heavens
with all their host, the earth and everything that
is on it, the seas and everything that is in them.
You give life to all of them, and the heavenly host
is bowing down to You.

Nehemiah 9:5-6 (AMP)

What power and might are Yours! Of course, You can restore and renew us. Of course You can silence Doug's enemies who speak out violence and death. *We know Your eyes are in every place watching the evil and the good in all their endeavors* (Proverbs 15:3 AMP). We bind, according to Matthew 16:18 (KJV), evil acts and words directed toward Doug. *We bind the perverse word which overwhelms, depresses and crushes the spirit. We bind harsh, painful and careless words that stir up anger. We permit only soft, gentle and thoughtful words which build up and encourage* (Proverbs 16:13, 21 AMP).

We release Your enduring loving kindness, mercy and grace to flood Doug's life so he can be a tree of life for his own children. Give him a glad heart. "You, Lord, are He who examines the motives and intent of his heart and You know the truth. You will vindicate him. It is by mercy, loving kindness and truth that evil is overcome" (Psalm 43:1 AMP).

Keep angels posted around Doug's family to protect and guide. Restore, restore, restore! *Give them ears that are quick to hear, eyes that see, minds that are quick to comprehend and hearts that understand* (Matthew 13:9-16 AMP). Restore them completely. Protect them from the evil one. We pray in the name of Jesus. Amen.

Prayer Thirty-Five

Abba Father, we know there's more to come. You haven't put us in the trash bin yet. We know how You use even our troubles to forge changes in us. We know even in times like this You will never shortchange us or bring us to shame (Romans 10:11 KJV).

You created family and You desire to restore this one. It may take trouble to rekindle our burned out lives with fresh hope. You restore dignity and respect to us and are on our side protecting us step by step. "In this world there are many troubles but You deliver us from them all" (John 16:33 AMP). We are so thankful.

Doug's court date is getting closer. Give him those "Aha" discoveries he needs to bring his case to a just conclusion. We ask You to help him find every document, text, photograph, bank statement, e-mail or other proof he needs to bring wrong-doing to light. Cause the enemy to return all that has been lost, stolen, and misplaced. Replace many times over all that is unjustly missing or destroyed. Give Doug grace in his victory. May his children see his kindness and compassion. Protect them and keep us all from the evil one. In the name of Jesus, Amen.

Prayer Thirty-Six

Abba Father, "There is no shadow of turning with You" (James 1:17 AMP). "You are the same yesterday, today and forever" (Hebrews 13:8 KJV). "Heaven and earth may pass away, but Your Word will never pass away" (Matthew 24:35 KJV). It is forever established in the heaven and is stable and sure (Psalm 119:89 KJV).

When You say Your thoughts are toward us and You plan for our good, we can really count on it (Jeremiah 29:11 KJV). When You tell us to put our trust in You, we really can. You will never let us down, never leave us, and never forsake us. *If we call to You, You will answer and tell us deep and mighty things we do not know* (Jeremiah 33:3 KJV).

We raise our prayers for Doug to Your Throne. He is a creative man who has experienced good success in many things. This season of trials and trouble has exhausted him, made him ill, tested his resolve and threatened his creativity. Release vitality, new ideas, new direction and new hope. Do more than restore him. *Make him into the man You designed him to be* (Ephesians 1:4 KJV). Enhance his gifts. Increase his productivity, build his faith and compassion and heal his body completely. We release new energy, happiness, gratitude and true love into his life.

Bless his children. Provide them with lots of things to laugh about. Give them respect for their father and a deep, intuitive understanding regarding what he's been through and what's been taken from him. Give them empathy and understanding. Protect them all and keep them from evil. We are grateful for Your kindness and love. We pray in the name of Jesus. Amen.

Prayer Thirty-Seven

Abba Father, When we think of the majesty of Your works we are more than in awe of You. "Your words and promises are pure, like silver refined in an earthen furnace, You keep and preserve them. Protect us from evil as vileness is exalted and baseness is prized by many" (Psalm 12:6-8 AMP). When we set our love upon You, You deliver us and set us on high (Psalm 91:14 KJV).

Thank You for restoring Doug and helping him on his journey. Thank You for clearing away obstacles and for uncovering what was previously hidden. Please expose false statements and false documents accumulated against him. Lead to truth those involved in this deception. Furnish the judge in Doug's case with a heart disposed toward full disclosure, restitution, and restoration. Set a love for truth and justice within the judge. Build Doug's case on truth upon truth. May Your wisdom rest upon him. We pray You will grant him gravitas, clarity, and charisma as he lays out his case.

We bind the wicked ways of Doug's opponents. Their sins will find them out. We release a spirit of repentance and remorse on them. We don't seek revenge, only justice. Today is the day for the truth.

Protect Doug and his family from the evil schemes, plots and plans laid around them. Free them from snares and lies and protect them from evil. We entreat You in the name of Jesus. Amen.

Prayer Thirty-Eight

Father, Thank You for eternal promises. "Not one word of all the good promises that the Lord had made to the house of Israel had failed, all came to pass" (Joshua 21:45 NIV). Your Word is certain and sure and forever established in the heavens (Psalm 119:89 KJV).

Thank You that we can count on Your Word and so are able to trust You to restore Doug. We "have been born again to an ever-living hope and inheritance which is beyond the reach of change or decay. It's unsullied and unfading, reserved in heaven for us" (1 Peter 1:3-9 KJV). What an amazing plan of salvation. Give us ever increasing faith to believe everything You say.

As Doug's court date approaches and the recovery of so much of what has been taken is at stake, we ask that the truth will be irrefutable. Guide the court to uncover and verify the facts. Command the evil one to restore to Doug those things taken from him. Let the scales of justice be balanced in the judge's decision making. Keep Your angels busy uncovering documents and removing obstacles along Doug's path.

We release Godly wisdom, quiet confidence, and a loving heart over Doug. Give him grace and just the right words to speak. We release breakthrough. *Thank You, that when the enemy comes in like a flood, You will raise a banner of love over Doug and his family* (Isaiah 59:19 KJV). We release protection and restoration in the name of Jesus. Amen.

Prayer Thirty-Nine

Abba Father, Blessed and adored be Your name, the
Father of mercies and the God of all comfort, who
comforts and encourages us in every trouble so that
we will be able to comfort and encourage others.
                              2 Corinthians 1:3-4 (AMP)

Your Word says whatever we ask in Your name believing we have received it, You will do it (Mark 11:24 KJV). *Whenever two or more are gathered, you are with us and hear us when we pray* (Matthew 18:20 KJV). *We are anxious for nothing and come boldly before Your Throne when we ask for help* (Hebrews 4:16 KJV).

Thank You for the privilege we have to bring our requests to You. Thank You for loving Doug so much that You chose us to keep his needs constantly before You. Thank You for Your personal plan for him. Thank You for calling him to loyalty and service to others. Thank You for giving him the heart of Daniel. He will be true to You and to his children no matter the cost. We release courage and honor, faith and steadfast love, honesty and truth for him. *We know it is truth that sets us free* (John 8:32 KJV), *love is stronger than death* (Romans 8:39 KJV), *and faith is the victory that overcomes the world* (1 John 5:4 KJV). Send the Holy Spirit to lead Doug and show him the way through the gauntlet before him.

"Bless the work of his hands and prosper him in all his works" (Deuteronomy 30:9 KJV). *We know that what the enemy means for harm You will use for good instead* (Genesis 50:20 KJV). Bind his heart to the heartbeat of his children and turn them toward their father. We trust You and know You are hard at work on Doug's behalf. We pray as instructed, in the name of Jesus. Amen.

Prayer Forty

Father God, "You change not, Your decrees and promises never fade or disappear" (Isaiah 40:3 KJV). We are so grateful You possess such a quality in Your character. Your purposes come to pass and Your plans will be accomplished.

You chose Doug from the beginning. Though he may feel his life is disappointing, You have had him in Your hand the entire time. Your plans for him have never wavered or changed. You have called him for such a time as this.

He has work to do, Lord. Complete his healing and continue to restore and repair his broken heart. End his loneliness and send him the Holy Spirit to be his Comforter. His children still need him and require his guidance. Do not allow them to be fatherless any longer. Reestablish this family. We release frank discussions, healing conversations and confident trust between Doug and his children. Bring them closer together than they have ever been. We release mutual respect and love among them.

We forbid interference from detractors and liars as Doug rebuilds his relationships and restores his family. We bind efforts to stifle or thwart truth, trust or healing. We release patience, wisdom, understanding, and discernment to Doug during this process. We have every confidence You will hear our prayers, grant him his heart's desire and protect him from the evil one. We pray in the name of Jesus. Amen.

Prayer Forty-One

Father God, You are our song and our salvation
(Psalm 188:14 KJV). You make a way where there
is no way (Isaiah 43 16:19 KJV). You feed us
when there is no food, heal us when there is no
hope and grant us victory when we stand defeated
before enemies too strong for us. Who is like You?
You reverse impossible situations and bring us
through fire and flood (Isaiah 43:2 KJV). You
know us.

Lord, protect and restore Doug. Let no further harm befall him. *Restore to him the years that the locusts have eaten* (Joel 2:25 NLT). We rebuke every lie told by "witnesses" in the past, in the present and in the future. We say when their mouths open they can only speak truth. Let demonic forces be disturbed, chaotic, and self destructive before the court. Let them fall on one another and expose what has been taking place. We ask you to restore for Doug every penny stolen, every moment taken, his health, and his tranquility. Restore his reputation. Let his children call him great, and regard him with respect and hearts of love. Restore his fortune and his good name. We thank You for Your goodness and kindness towards us. Receive our prayers in the name of Jesus. Amen.

Prayer Forty-Two

The Word of God is operative, energizing and effective. It is sharper than any two edged sword, penetrating the deepest parts of our nature, exposing and judging the very thoughts and intentions of the heart. Not a creature exists that is concealed from His sight, but all things are open and exposed and revealed to the eyes of Him with whom we have to give account.

Hebrews 4:12-13 (AMP)

Jesus, You are the Word made flesh. You are the living Word, Who came for a time to dwell among us (John 1:12 AMP). *You granted us the ability to come boldly before You to ask for help in our time of need* (Hebrews 4:16 AMP). Thank You.

Restore to Doug all he needs in every area of his life. *Teach him to rely on You and to put his hope in those things which are unseen, but eternal* (2 Corinthians 4:18 AMP). Whoever puts his trust and confidence in You will be exalted and safe. *You have given Doug power, love, and a sound mind, not a spirit of fear* (2 Timothy 1:7 KJV).

Remove any fear of what man might do (Proverbs 29:25 KJV).*Who can be against him when You are on his side* (Romans 8:31 KJV)? Deliver him and set him high above his enemies. Release peace and restore his joy. We lift our prayer in the name of Jesus. Amen.

Prayer Forty-Three

"All my bones say, Lord who is like You, Who rescues the afflicted from him who is too strong for him to resist alone, and the afflicted and needy from him who robs him" (Psalm 35:10 AMP)?

Malicious witnesses rise up against Doug and repay him evil for good, to the sorrow of his soul (Psalm 31:40 AMP). "Like godless jesters at a feast they gnash at Doug with their teeth in malice" (Psalm 35:16 AMP). Don't let those who are wrongfully Doug's enemies rejoice over him.

> How long will You look on without acting? Rescue Doug's life, his only life, from their destructions and we will give You thanks; they devise deceitful words, half truths and lies against him. You have seen this O Lord; do not keep silent. Do not be far from him. Wake Yourself up and arise to his right and to his cause; You are his God and his Lord. Do not let them rejoice over him. Do not let them say in their heart, 'Aha, this is what we wanted. We have swallowed him up and destroyed him. ' Let them be ashamed and humiliated who rejoice at his distress. Let them be clothed with shame and dishonor who magnify themselves over him. Let them be turned back in defeat and dishonored who delight in his hurt. Psalm 35:16,17, 19-23 (AMP; Doug added)

"Let them shout for joy and rejoice, who favor Doug's vindication, and want what is right for him" (Psalm 35: 27 AMP). *(Doug added)*.

Incline to us and hear our cry. Bring Doug out of the pit which his enemies dug for him and set his feet upon a rock, steady his footsteps and establish his path. Put a new song in his heart, a song of praise. You are pleased with a man who does not regard the proud nor the liar, and who regards Your wonderful deeds. Psalm 40:2-17 (AMP; Doug added)

Continue to show Doug mercy and goodness, and blessing and favor we pray in the name of Jesus. Amen.

Prayer Forty-Four

In the Mighty name of Jesus, the Name above all names, the Name which conquers all, in every circumstance and situation. His is the Name of surpassing victory (Ephesians 1:21 AMP).

Restore Doug and let him say "I am strong"(Joel 3:10 AMP). Place Your hand on him and let him say "I am loved"(John 3:16 KJV). Speak to him and let him say "there is nothing too hard for my God" (Jeremiah 32:27 KJV). *I am strong in the power of His might* (2 Corinthians 12:10 KJV). Allow these truths to soak into every cell of his being with weighty certainty. Enable him to walk in Your peace. You, O God, put him under the shadow of Your wings and keep him safe. Be his shield and comfort, his Father, and his friend. Reverse every damaged cell and every painful or distorted aspect of his life, we pray. Amen.

Chapter Eleven

Prayers Forty-Five to Fifty-Five

Some boast in chariots and some in horses, but
we will boast in the name of the Lord, our God.
They have bowed down and fallen, but we have
risen and stood upright.

__ Psalm 20:7-8 *(NIV)*

Prayer Forty-Five

Father, Thank You that You never leave or forsake us (Deuteronomy 31:6 KJV). Thank You for being steadfast and sure though storms of every kind may rage around us. Thank You for keeping us whether we are going through famine or flood, through plenty or want.

We know the devil really hates that we continue to pray for Doug. He is trying to strike out against all of us, but You are so far greater than he is (1 John 4:4 KJV). You are the Creator of all things (Colossians 1:16 AMP). We put our hope and trust in You. These battle signs tell us we are close to breakthrough so we are pushing on to victory. We have made our requests for Doug known to You again and again and we know You are going to act on his behalf.

Please protect our little team. They are mighty warriors, but even the mighty can suffer wounds. We release perfect health and protection over all involved. We take authority over all the power of the enemy (Luke 10:19 KJV) and forbid him to act counter to Your purposes.

Please act on Doug's behalf right now. Please imbue him with power from on high (Luke 24:49 KJV). Fill his life with the gifts and fruits which come from the Holy Spirit. Grant him Your perspective and wisdom. Release discernment so he can easily perceive what is hidden from the eye.

Hedge him in. Protect him and keep Your angels close at hand to guard and guide. We pray in the name of Jesus. Amen.

Prayer Forty-Six

Jesus, You are the Lily of the Valley, The bright and Morning Star, the Wonderful Counselor, The Prince of Peace (Revelation 22:16 KJV). All Power in Heaven and Earth belongs to You and yet You intercede for us

(Matthew 28:18 KJV). Thank You for being our Redeemer and our Friend. You are the Light of the World and our hope resides in Your finished Work.

Thank You for loving Doug so much and for carrying him safely through each and every difficulty in his entire life. *Thank You for taking his present trials, and turning what the devil meant for harm, into something good* (Genesis 50:20 KJV). Thank You for setting Your hand upon him to calm him and bring him heart peace. Thank You for binding Your heart to his. We declare wisdom and understanding for him. *We release health, justice, reparation and restoration to every area of his life* (Job 1:10 KJV). We bind greed, deceit, lies and evil schemes planned by the adversary. They are forbidden in heaven and on earth.

We ask You to tie the hearts of Doug's children to his heart with strong cords of love and respect. Hedge them in, hide them and keep them from the evil one. In the name of Jesus, Amen.

Prayer Forty-Seven

Worthy are You, O Lord to receive glory and honor, wisdom and strength, knowledge and power (Revelation 5:12 AMP). You are great in mercy and loving kindness and You give good gifts to Your children (Luke 11:13 KJV). Everything within us blesses and praises Your Holy Name.

We know You have set Your thoughts upon Doug and You have called him from a sea of lost hopes to bring him to Your side. You've done this so he will come to know the sound of Your still small voice speaking to him in the night. You've done it because You have always known him and longed for his companionship. *You've done it because You want Your plans for his good to be realized* (Jeremiah 29:11 AMP).

We release blessings of hope, peace, patience, health, understanding, wisdom and joy to our brother. We loose kind and calming speech in him, through him and around him. We loose laughter and happiness.

Restore Doug and his family in perfect Shalom. We go into the enemy's camp and we take back what the devil has stolen. He doesn't get to keep it.

We worship and thank You for hearing our prayers. In the name of Jesus we pray. Amen.

Prayer Forty-Eight

Blessed by Grace and compassion is he who considers the helpless; the Lord will save him in the day of trouble. The Lord will protect him and keep him alive; the Lord will sustain him and restore him to health.

Psalm 41:11-3 (AMP)

Today is the day of salvation and deliverance, the day of breakthrough and peace for Doug. We remind You how he has always had compassion on the helpless. *We thank You for going before him, standing beside him and being his rear guard* (Psalm 139:5 AMP). No tactic or strategy against him will succeed. *You will deliver him from the hands of the enemy because you have set Your love upon him* (Psalm 91:14 KJV). *It is your kind intent to give him blessings* (Ephesians 1:3-5 KJV).

Surround him and his children and enfold them in Your love. Keep them from every trap and snare. Protect their hearts and keep them safe from those who destroy with action or word. Our trust and hope is in You. Restore Doug to all that is taken from him and grant him joy and strength. We pray in the name of Jesus. Amen.

Prayer Forty-Nine

Lord, We want Doug to see how much You love him, how You speak of Him to the very angels of heaven (Luke 4:10 KJV). We want him to see You have never turned Your back on him and have no intention of doing so now (Hosea 6:1 KJV).

We are down to the wire! Doug is on his way to court to make his case and petition. We have prayed, believed, hoped, and asked for Your divine intervention. *We know You hate injustice and wrong doing, so allow truth and justice to come forth* (Isaiah 61:8 KJV).

Set right in court the wrongs done to Doug. Set them right in heaven. Set them right on earth. "But let justice run down like water and righteousness like a mighty stream" (Amos 5:24 NKJV). We know You will. Give Doug peace and fill him with strength and joy. Turn the hearts of his children to him in love and set their angels round about to guard, guide and assist them. Protect them from the schemes of the enemy and place their feet on the road to liberty in You. We make our requests in the name of Jesus. Amen.

Prayer Fifty

Abba Father, You are faithful, reliable, trustworthy and ever true to Your promises. You can be depended upon. You will keep Doug to the end, keeping him free of accusation (1 Corinthians 1:8-9 AMP). We know You are wise; the wisdom of the world is foolishness to You (1 Corinthians 3:19 AMP); You are strong; far beyond the limits of human strength or effort.

We have no boast of our own, we only boast in You (1 Corinthians 10:17 AMP). You know all and see all. You have already sorted the end from the beginning *Your call cannot be revoked or annulled (Romans 11:29 KJV).* Your plan for Doug's health and restoration and that for his children will stand and no human hand can stop it or derail it. We trust You.

Father, we put You in remembrance of your child Doug, who has humbled himself to accept all these prayers and intercession. He has quietly received each and every prayer, not resisting or exhibiting pride. He has agreed with us as we pray for changes in his life and has not inserted his personal agenda, nor requested a single prayer contradicting Your Word. *He has shown his heart and his hunger for the living water that flows from You* (John 7:38 NIV). He has exhibited his hope for change, his longing to hear from You and his need for things to change. *You do not despise a broken and contrite heart* (Psalm 51:17 NLT). You will answer our cries. We have every confidence in You.

We are looking forward to Doug receiving justice, restoration and restitution. Most of all, we look forward to him being reunited with his children and living his life as the loving, caring father he longs to be.

Thank You for being faithful even when we aren't. Deliver and save him today we pray, in the name of Jesus. Amen.

Prayer Fifty-One

Abba Father, thank You for Your mighty power and Your steadfast love. You are more than we could imagine, "the Fairest of Ten Thousand" (Song of Solomon 5:10 KJV). You are from the beginning, The I AM (Exodus 3:14 KJV). You are the Everlasting God who made all things (Isaiah 40:28 KJV). Thank You for consenting to hear us when we pray.

Let our prayers for Doug and his family be heard on high. Allow them to rise before You like incense. Hear us when we ask for help on his behalf. Please keep Your focus on him and his needs. We know in You there is surpassing victory. *You are the author and finisher of our faith* (Hebrews 12:2 KJV). You will perfect all things concerning Doug. *You will direct his paths and give him the desires of his heart* (Psalm 37:4-5 KJV). *Bless and protect him and bring his case before heaven's court* (Psalm 82:1 KJV). Please release restoration and justice for Doug. Bring him restoration, peace which passes understanding, joy, and abiding love for You. In the name of Jesus, accept our prayer. Amen.

Prayer Fifty-Two

Abba Father, "You have set before us blessings and curses, life and death. Today we choose life that we may live" (Deuteronomy 30:19 KJV). We choose blessings and gratitude, faith and trust. We choose what is good and true and right and just. We choose those things that are invisible yet eternal (2 Corinthians 4; 18 NIV).

Thank You for all the gifts You have given Your children. We appreciate our angelic guards and warring angels, we appreciate being hidden under the shadow of Your wing. We appreciate the saving grace of Jesus and the promise of eternity with You.

Our trials and hardships are fleeting and temporary, yet You care about them and about each of us (2 Corinthians 4:17 NIV). You have set Your heart on Doug and his situation. You are calling to him and delivering him from the grasp of the evil one. You are bringing him from slavery to son-ship and setting him at liberty for the remainder of his life. *You have granted him every blessing in the spiritual realm* (Ephesians 1:3 AMP).

Thank you. Bring him all the way out to freedom, peace and joy. In the name of Jesus, Amen.

Prayer Fifty-Three

"For I am the Lord thy God who takes hold of your right hand and says to you, 'Do not fear, I will help you'"(Isaiah 41:13 KJV).

Thank you Father, "Every good and perfect gift comes from Your hand" (James 1:17 KJV). *Thank You for establishing us in countries and families and communities that are just what we need to develop into the people you want us to be* (Acts 17:26 AMP). *No matter how dismal it looks to us, You are always changing what the devil means for harm to our good and for the saving of many* (Genesis 50:20 KJV). Thank You for the good and the bad, the simple and the complex, the easy and the difficult. We need it all in order to become what You designed us to be. Bolster us when times are tough and remind us it's You when times are great. Thank You.

Doug is looking forward to the day of deliverance, the day when the grasping, lying and self serving tall tales will come to an end. We release over him the endurance he needs for this last mile. We release realistic outcomes, steadfast love and godly wisdom. *Give him vision to see through any hoax or lie, courage to be fair to himself in the process, and bright hope for his future* (Psalm 119:66 KJV). We release health of mind and body, repayment, restoration and restitution. We release forgiveness, the end to harmful hostility, and a solution in his favor.

Give him peace and trust in You as You show him how You will put things right for him. Pour Your love upon, in and around him today. We pray in the name of Jesus. Amen.

Prayer Fifty-Four

Father God, You are a faithful God, never changing, wavering or quitting. You keep Your Word. Your character is defined by doing what You have said You will do. We can count on You (Deuteronomy 7:9 KJV). "You are not a man that You should lie" (Numbers 23:19 KJV). It's such a relief to know You are always true and on our side (Psalm 119:7 KJV).

You are the very definition of justice, mercy, fairness, balance, love, light, goodness, kindness and self control. You will not bring Doug to shame because You are on his side and want the best for him. You are planning everything he needs for breakthrough and restoration. *You will deliver him from the hands of his adversaries* (2 Samuel 22:1 KJV). Bring Doug a victory in the doctor's office, the courtroom, the negotiating chamber, or wherever he might be. Break the chains that have been placed around him and restore his liberty in body, mind, and spirit.

Keep angels at his side and next to his children, as You guide them and protect them from the evil one. We pray in the name of Jesus, believing You will hear and answer us. Amen.

Prayer Fifty-Five

"The Lord upholds all who are falling and raises up all who are bowed down" (Psalm 145:19 NLT). "You abound in mercy and loving kindness; ever ready to be gracious to your people" (Psalm 86:5 KJV). You hung the stars and yet You give thought to us (Job 9:9 KJV). You are kind and gracious (Psalm 145:9-9 KJV). Thank you.

We are trusting in You to bless and keep Doug. *We know You chose him as your own before the World was made* (Ephesians 1:4 AMP). You have chased him down, hold him in Your hand and desire great things for him. You will not leave or forsake him but will rather see Your plan for his life realized.

Keep him hedged in and safe as he takes the last steps in this phase of his life. *Bless and prosper him and vindicate him* (Isaiah 62:3 KJV). Let every wagging tongue be proved wrong and reverse every curse spoken over his life. Keep him beneath Your wing and safe from every plot and plan of the devil. Give him the desires of his heart we pray in the name of Jesus. Amen.

Chapter Twelve

Prayers Fifty-Six through Sixty-Four

No weapon forged against you will prevail, and you will refute every tongue that accuses you. This is the heritage of the servants of the Lord, and this is their vindication from me, declares the Lord.

__Isaiah 54:17 *(NLT)*

Prayer Fifty-Six

Jesus Savior, You are seated at the right hand of God (Luke 22:69 KJV). You are worthy, able, persistent, funny, kind, loyal, trustworthy, patient, royal, and wise. You love us and long to make us what we need to be. You can do far beyond and exceedingly above all we could ever ask or think (Ephesians 3:30 AMP).

You take action on our behalf and You will bring us to life eternal. We have nothing to compare to Your love and light.

Reach out Your hand and answer Doug. Return hope and expectation to his life. Turn Your face toward him and show him Your favor. *Speak to him clearly and call to him in the night so he will see how amazingly personal You are* (1 Samuel 3:8 KJV). Mend the fragments of his shattered heart and put the finishing touches of healing in place. In Your flawless timing return to him those things he treasures.

Bless and keep his children. Guide them in the way eternal, soften their hearts and instill in them a longing to spend time and effort on their relationship with Doug. Bring peace and joy to each of them as You bring a new light to their path. *Illuminate their darkness* (John 1:9 KJV).

We ask these things in the name of Jesus. Amen.

Prayer Fifty-Seven

Abba Father, We "have need of endurance so that when we have done the will of God we may receive what was promised" (Hebrews 10:36). "We have been rejoicing in hope, persevering in tribulation and devoted to prayer" (Romans 12:12 KJV). Hear us as we call to You for breakthrough in Doug's situation.

You know every dream, both dreams realized and dreams waiting to be born. You know every sadness and joy, every expectation, disappointment, triumph, hurt and loss. When we pray for Doug, we are praying for someone you already know well.

You are true to Your promises. Where could one go to find a God like You? Thank You for calling us to pray for Doug and rally round him in his hour of need. We know You love him and have him in Your heart. We release from heaven: health, restoration, reparation, resolve, and recompense. *We release the ability to look at those things which are unseen, but are true and real. We loose spiritual discernment and truth* (1 Corinthians 2:15 NIV). Allow him to immediately tell truth from fiction. We prohibit stall tactics and sabotage from dictating how he lives his life.

We ask You every day to come to his rescue and defense, because You told us to ask and keep on asking (Matthew 7:7 KJV). We are asking because we care about his heart and we care about his state of mind. When we say "peace" for him, we know how much he needs peace. When we pray "restoration," it's because we know what he's lost and the pain and despair it's caused. We are interceding for him day after day because you asked us to. We're bringing to your remembrance all our prayers since the beginning and asking you to act now. *Give him the sign he needs so he can be confident in Your goodness and mercy and Your justice and grace* (Psalm 23:6 KJV). In the name of Jesus we pray. Amen.

Prayer Fifty-Eight

O God, do not keep silent, for the mouth of the wicked and the mouth of the deceitful are opened against Doug. They have spoken against him with a lying tongue; they have also surrounded him with words of hatred and have fought against him without a cause. In return for his love, they attack him, but He is in prayer. They have repaid him evil for good and hatred for his love.

Psalm 109: 1-5 (AMP)

"But You O Lord, show kindness to *Doug* for Your name's sake; Your loving kindness is good, O Lord rescue him; for he is suffering and needy and his heart is wounded within him" (Psalm 109:21-22 AMP).

Help Doug, O Lord my God; save him according to Your loving kindness and let him know this is Your hand; it's You, Lord who has done it. Let them curse, but You bless. When adversaries arise, let them be ashamed, but let Your servant rejoice, let his attackers be covered with dishonor, and let them cover themselves with their own shame as a robe.

Psalm 109: 26-29 *(AMP)*

Doug "will give great praise and thanks to the Lord with his mouth; and in the midst of many He will praise You, for You will stand at his right hand to save him from those who judge his soul" (Psalm 109: 30 AMP).

You are able to do far above anything we can ask or think. You are able to restore Doug and all things concerning him.

We do not ask in vain to one who cannot hear. Our prayers are to the true and living God. You are He who rides through the heavens to our help. You hear when we cry to You. You are bent on saving us from our troubles. You rejoice over our victories and bring us to safety. *Give us cause to rejoice in Your faithful deliverance* (Deuteronomy 33:26-29 NIV). We thank You, in the name of Jesus, the Messiah. Amen.

Prayer Fifty-Nine

The Lord lives, blessed be my Rock and exalted be my God, the Rock of my salvation. He brings me out from my enemies and even lifts me above those who rise up against me. His covenant with us is everlasting, ordered in all things and secured. For will He not cause to grow and prosper all my salvation and my every wish? Will He not cause them to grow and be prosperous? See below 1 Samuel 21, 22 (AMP)

How could we possibly ask for, expect or yearn for more than You have already so freely offered? *This is why we pray with great confidence, knowing Doug already has restoration as his present possession* (Mark 11:24 NIV). We are waiting with great expectation for everything to come to pass as we have asked. *We rest in the certainty of Your promises to him and wait for You in peace because we know You have perfect timing in meeting all of his needs and requests* (Hebrews 6:15-20 AMP). Be especially close to him. Let him feel Your Presence and see Your angels as they take position over his house and around his bed. *Assure him he is safe and has no need for alarm. You will keep him, sustain him and give him grace and strength* (Psalm 121:7 AMP).

Bring his children to him quickly. They will be grown soon and would benefit from being with him now. In the name of Jesus we pray. Amen.

Prayer Sixty

"Listen to my Prayer O God and do not hide yourself from my plea. Listen to and answer me. {Doug} is restless and distraught in his complaint and distracted because of the voice of the enemy, because of the pressure of the wicked; for they bring down trouble on him and in their anger persecute him. Confuse his enemies and let them speak to the magistrates with both sides of their mouth and get trapped in their own venom and lies. These are people with which {Doug} used to have sweet fellowship.

Psalm 55:1-3, 9, 14 (AMP)

As for Doug,

We will call upon God and the Lord will save him. We will complain evening and morning and noon and He will hear us. He will redeem his life in peace from the battles against him, for there are many. God will hear and humble them, He who sits enthroned from old, because in his enemies there has been no change of heart. Psalm 55;16-18 (AMP)

If we cast Doug's burdens upon You, You will uphold and sustain him. You will never allow him to slip, fall or fail. You are faithful to deliver him from all his troubles (Psalm 55:19-22 AMP).

In You O Lord we place our trust and faith. We have no fear. What can man do to us? This we know: God is for us (Psalm 56:11-12 KJV).

Direct Doug's steps and order his plans (Proverbs 16:9 KJV). Bring his settlement to a conclusion which accrues to his good. Do Your good will for him. Protect him from evil. In the name of Jesus we pray. Amen.

Prayer Sixty-One

Abba Father, "You are the same yesterday, today and forever. All things may pass away but Your Word will never pass away" (Luke 21:33 KJV). Your plans and purposes for everything will be realized and Your name will be confessed by all. Every knee will bow to Your Lordship (Philippians 2:10 KJV).

Teach us how to bow O Lord. We are not good at it. We want our own way. We are strong headed and willful. Teach us to bow. We could save ourselves so much trouble!

I place Your son Doug before You and ask You to be his perfect, well timed, never late help in his time of trouble (Psalm 46:1-2 KJV). Hear his heart's cry and act on his behalf. We contend for good news on his behalf. Provide him wisdom in all his dealings, the ability to understand and discern even the most complex situations. Give him creative solution skills, articulate expression and a loving heart. Let his words exhort and heal all those with whom he has dealings. *Hide him away from the wicked one under the shadow of Your wing where no evil can befall him* (Psalm 91:1-2 KJV). Deliver him from his enemies.

Surround his loved ones with angelic guards and give them discernment and wisdom. We ask these things in the name of Jesus. Amen.

Prayer Sixty-Two

Abba Father, "You are the great and mighty, the terrible God. Even Your enemies know You are fierce and awesome and different from all other gods" (Nehemiah 9:32 KJV). You are the God who ever lives and who knows the end from the beginning (Isaiah 46:10 KJV). Hold out Your hand of mercy just a little longer, we pray.

You say "no one who trusts in you will ever be disgraced, but disgrace comes to those who try to deceive others" (Psalm 25:3-5 KJV). Lord we agree with you; make it so. "You desire to see a mighty flood of justice, a river of righteous living that never will run dry" (Amos 5:24 NIV). You want Doug to emerge victorious from his trials. You want him to be refined and purified by the fire he's been walking through. We know You will bring him through the flames intact. We know You are ready to hear our prayers and bless him. You are ready to grant us our requests.

We are alert to Your warnings. We know to watch out for attacks from the devil, our great enemy. We take a firm stand against him. We don't wage war with human plans and methods. We use God's mighty weapons, not mere worldly weapons, to knock down the devil's strongholds. We pull down the stronghold over Doug's finances, his family, all those who conspire against him, in the name of Jesus. No plan of the enemy will succeed. Nothing can prevent his restoration. Amen.

Prayer Sixty-Three

Abba Father, we ascribe all glory and honor to You. It is Your grace that saved us and Your love which transforms us. You have brought us into companionship with You, we are robed in Your righteousness, not our own, and we thank You.

May You grant Doug out of the riches of Your glory, to be strengthened and spiritually energized with power through the Spirit in his inner self. May he be deeply rooted and fully grounded in love so that he is able to comprehend the width and length and height and depth of Your love for him. Give him the richest experience of Your love so that he will come to know the joy of Your Presence. You can do infinitely beyond all of Doug's hopes, dreams and prayers and super abundantly more than he dares think or ask because of Your power at work within him.
Ephesians 3:16-19 *(AMP;* Doug added)

We trust You to hear and answer our requests and believe that You are accomplishing Your will in Doug's situation. We are grateful You are at work to restore and reinstate all he has lost. Please continue to protect his children; unite them in love to their father. Protect them from the prince of darkness and lead them in pathways of truth and light. In the name of Jesus we pray. Amen.

Prayer Sixty-Four

Father, We exalt You. You are exalted in all the earth (Psalm 30:1 KJV). You have led us out of darkness into Your marvelous light (1 Peter 2.9 KJV).

You lead us forth with Your right hand of righteousness. We do not fear. We know You will protect us and even pick us up when necessary to carry us away from the defeat the enemy has planned. You have rescued us from so great a threat of death, and will continue to rescue us. On You we have set our hope. You will again rescue us from danger and draw us near.

Isaiah 41:10-12 (KJV)

Thank You for all You have done for Doug. *Deep calls to deep so we pray Doug will hear Your call and come to know the sound of Your voice* (John 10:27 KJV). Give him a heart of peace and a spirit of joy. Show him Your deliverance and restore his family and fortunes. *Don't withhold any good thing from him, rather pour out Your grace and favor* (Psalm 84:9-12 NIV). Continue to build his hope, his trust in You, his joy, his discernment, and his perseverance.

You are a God of breakthrough and You are with him right now. Break through the hearts of his children; break through the walls of greed, jealousy and destruction surrounding them. "Cry out, O Lord, from the high places and shatter the strongholds of our enemies" (Psalm 69: 1-4 NLT). Give Doug those things for which his soul yearns and his heart desires.

Grant him Your Shalom and be his God of comfort and solace. With thanksgiving, expectancy, and gratitude we ask in the name of Jesus. Amen.

Chapter Fourteen
Prayer Sixty-five to Seventy

And I will make you to this people a fortified wall of bronze; they will fight against you, but they will not prevail over you, for I am with you always to save you and protect you says the Lord.

_Jeremiah 15:20 *(AMP)*

Prayer Sixty-Five

Abba Father, We thank You for every step forward, for every breath that fills our lungs, for every moment of life, for every incremental victory we experience.

We know without doubt we will prevail, for we are persuaded that You will keep that which we committed to You until the very end. Doug will prevail, he will be restored (2 Timothy 1:12 KJV). He will find true happiness and joy. He will be at peace. His finances will be multiplied beyond his reckoning. Thank You so much. We are standing with him; we are waiting and watching with great expectation as his triumph approaches.

Make today the final move for Doug's enemies, their last play. His cause is just and righteous. He's only asking for truth and justice. *Send angels to fight next to him. Father, one of Your angels was able to slay 185,000 enemy troops in a single night* (2 Kings 19:35 KJV). It will be so easy for You to dispatch the help He needs. *There is nothing too hard for You; nothing* (Jeremiah 32:27 KJV). Please act on Doug's behalf. You can change hearts with one encounter. You can bring remorse, shame and repentance to all his enemies.

Restore this family and keep the children safely gathered in Your arms. Please talk to them. Comfort them. Advise them. Speak to them while they sleep. Send angels to watch over them and keep them from the plans and schemes the devil has for them. Heal them completely. They have a place in Your eternal Kingdom. We aren't willing to face eternity without them, so let them know You are alive, real, and ready to restore them.

We bring our requests boldly; full of confidence that You will say "Yes" to every request (Hebrews 4:16 KJV). In the name of Jesus we pray. Amen.

Prayer Sixty-Six

The Lord God helps me therefore I am not disgraced.
I have set my face like a flint and I know I shall
not be put to shame; he who vindicates Doug is
near. Who will contend with Doug? We will stand
up together. Who are Doug's adversaries? Let them
go ahead and confront him for it is the Lord God
who helps him; who will declare him guilty? You
are his deliverer.

Psalm 50:7-9 (AMP: Doug added))

Lord, act on Doug's behalf. You have heard our cries and You know the state of his inmost being. You know the state of every heart. You know every hurt, every damaging word spoken, every curse, every wicked plot and plan. You are the One who delivers and heals. It is through You that these fractures and pains can be reversed and restoration can take place. Please act on behalf and in favor of Doug's complete restoration. We bind and forbid the destructive and harsh word, the disagreeable and greedy actions, and the lies and deception. We release happiness and a full and abundant life to him. Thank You for Your grace, kindness, patience and love. In the name of Jesus we pray. Amen.

Prayer Sixty-Seven

Father God, Our ways are not hidden from You. You know our thoughts from far off and our words before we speak them (Psalm 139:4 KJV). You know the number of our days, so short, compared to our eternity.

You press us on every side because You want us to choose You. You challenge and upset us so we will become what You need us to be. You give us jobs we can't figure out how to perform and put us in situations that seem impossible to get through. But, it's in our weakness You show Yourself mighty and strong. *When we can no longer stand, You rise up and fight on our behalf* (Isaiah 40:28-29 KJV). We just have to move out of our own way. Remind us to move quickly so You can work. Thank You for all the times You have acted to defend and help us.

We release Shalom to Doug. As he waits in peace for the miracles we seek on his behalf, we release assurance of his victory, wise counselors, and companions who speak truth to him. You say, "Hope deferred makes the heart sick, but a promise fulfilled is a tree of life" (Proverbs 13:12 KJV). We release answered prayers and hope fulfilled. Restore Doug as we pray. *Change his sorrow to gladness and his sadness to joy* (John 16:16-24).

Consider too, the fate of his children. They need him to teach them how to navigate the storms of life. They need his comfort, provision, and leadership; all the things kids need from a father. Repair and restore these relationships in full measure.

Guard them all from the evil one. Set up defenses in the eye and ear so they will easily see and hear truth. Give them discernment and wisdom so they can sort out these emotional and complex issues. Cause the deceiver to identify him/herself. Let the lies come to the surface and be found out. Raise Your hand to defend this family. Thank You for hearing and answering this prayer. In the name of Jesus, hear us, we pray. Amen.

Prayer Sixty Eight

Father God, Thank You so much that Your love for us is stronger than life and stronger than death. Nothing in this world or the world to come can take us away from You (Romans 8:38 KJV). You won't allow it. You have called us by name.

You have written Doug's name in Your book, You know him (Psalm 139:16 KJV). We really count on this promise. We find our peace in You. You won't let anything take us away from You. *We are safe and secure in Your Everlasting Arms* (Deuteronomy 33:27 KJV). What a great Father You are!

We are bringing Doug's situation to You yet again because he's a good father too. He calls his children by name and he knows them. He has plans for them, for their good. He wants the best for them. He cannot imagine letting them go. You made him like You in so many ways. You know exactly what this has been like for him. You know the pain, the longing, the nights of rehearsing in his head what he'd say if he had the chance. You know. It must break Your heart too. But Lord, all things are possible with You, so You can change things. You can send angels to speak to mankind. You can intervene. You can turn what the devil means for bad into good. Please restore to Doug all the rights and responsibilities of fatherhood. Don't let another night go by where these children are separated from their father's love. Bring them home, we pray.

We petition the courts of heaven to rule on Doug's behalf. Hear our petition for him in the court of heaven as You did in the days of Daniel. *Send Your messenger angels to carry out the court's decree and set things right* (1 Kings 22:19-23 KJV).

We petition and pray in the name of Jesus; the Name above all names. Amen.

Prayer Sixty-Nine

Father God, There are times when we come to You so tired and strained, with so many cares pressing us, it feels impossible to praise You or thank You. Even so, You deserve all praise whether the day is good or bad, You are so good to us.

You have given us such plenty. We have free time, choices, a roof over us, food in the pantry. Our furniture is padded; we can decide what to wear. We abound in every material thing while most of the world does not. Thank You for our blessings and the abundance You have given us. Thank You for hearing us when we pray and telling us how to pray in the first place. *Thank You for adopting us and seating us with You in heavenly* places (Ephesians 1: 19-20 KJV). Thank You for friends and family and for all the beauty with which we daily are surrounded. Grant us Your peace.

We know You are arranging all things for Doug's good (Romans 8:28 KJV). *You have plans for him and will see him through* (Romans 11:36 KJV). Give him cause for joy and give him hope. Act on his behalf; hear the cries of our heart as we seek You for the answer. In the name of Jesus we pray. Amen.

Prayer Seventy

Abba Father, "Righteousness and justice are the foundation of Your throne" (Psalm 89:14 KJV). What amazing words these are. I looked them up. You built Your throne on principles that call on man to live on the highest plane of existence.

Righteousness and justice are two words we hear all the time, but we don't think about the meaning. This describes the qualities that make Your authority and sovereignty completely valid. Thank You so much for being the righteous and just God of all the worlds.

When we ask for justice for Doug, it's because he has chosen to walk in Your righteousness. We are asking You to set him free to live the life You intended for him. Cause him to be able to make the decisions You ordained. He is not vindictive, not wanting to get even; he just wants justice. We release justice in heaven and justice on earth. We release his ability to walk out the righteous life You've called him to. We know wherever Doug falls short, You will display Your famous mercy and restore him.

You are gracious Lord, and abounding in mercy and loving kindness (Psalm 103:8 KJV). *Thank You for being who You are, perfect in all Your ways* (Psalm 18:30 KJV). Restore and heal our friend so that we may praise You in the great assembly. In the name of Jesus, we pray. Amen.

Prayer Seventy-One

The Lord is my best friend and my shepherd, I always have more than enough. He offers a resting place for me in his luxurious love. His tracks take me to an oasis of peace, the quiet brook of bliss. That's where he restores and revives my life. He opens before me pathways to God's pleasure and leads me along in his footsteps of righteousness, so that I can bring honor to his name. Lord, even when your pathway takes me through the deepest darkness, fear will never conquer me, for I have You. You remain close to me and lead me. You are near. You fill me to overflowing, your goodness and love pursue me all the days of my life. After, I'll dwell with You forever.

Psalm 23: 1-6 (Passion Translation)

Thank You, Lord, that all Your promises to restore us to peace and joy are true and irrefutable. Thank You that You hear and answer our prayers. Thank You for Your mercy and kindness and for the love you so freely lavished upon us through Your Holy Son. We have seen You acting on Doug's behalf and we are grateful. "And now O Lord, for what do I wait? My hope is in you" (Psalms 39:7 KJV). Praise the Name of the Lord. Amen.

Conclusion

At the moment the pandemic of Covid-19 is sweeping across the world. In many places, people are confined to their homes, only allowed out for food or medicine. I live in the New York metro area, and see first hand the devastation caused by thousands of deaths, the boarded up businesses, the closed hair salons, restaurants, and corner dry cleaners. I have no idea whether or not these little businesses will survive the lock-down. We don't know what the future of our communities will be like, but we know it will be changed.

Now, more than ever since World War II, we need to carry the great hope that restoration is possible. Lost income, lost dreams, deferred or disappeared plans, and especially the untimely death of loved ones, all contribute to the need to rebuild and be restored to what was before. Schools are closed and we don't know for how long. Even businesses that are open are operating under restrictions and rules never before in place. Restoration doesn't really seem possible, does it? The past is water under the bridge, and the future more uncertain than ever. Is there anything dependable?

This little book about restoration recognizes that sometimes circumstances beyond our control can and do happen. Our need for a miracle can be thrust upon us through no doing of our own. Such is the case right now for many of us. We don't know when or how to start rebuilding our lives.

What are we supposed to do and where do we turn? There

may be some government financial assistance, a mental health hotline to call, a food bank to assist with putting food on the table. But where does one go to address the dreams now dashed, the plans that won't be realized, the opportunities lost? We aren't the first generation to encounter challenges, some much more grave than this one. Even now it's not just the corona virus taking dreams away: there are clashing ethnic groups, religious persecution, and regional instability of all kinds creating even more desperate situations for many. Refugees are flooding into Europe by the thousands, each with his or her own story of personal loss and harm.

All around us things seem to change, at best, and devolve, at the worst. What do we do? There is no easy answer, but there is an answer. It may not even be the answer you want, but it is the answer. It may seem sophomoric, ethereal, unpopular or politically incorrect, but it remains the ultimate answer. You may not want it to be true, but the fact does not change. The answer you seek is God. He is the only One who can work outside of time to restore you. He is the only One who can erase your past, transform your present and insure your future. He's the only one who can return to you something that is gone.

> I look up to the mountains-does my help come from there?
> My help comes from the Lord, who made heaven and earth!
> He will not let you stumble;
> The One who watches over you will not slumber,
> Indeed, He who watches over Israel never slumbers or sleeps.
> The Lord himself watches over you!
> The Lord stands beside you as your protective shade.
> The sun will not harm you by day, nor the moon at night.

The Lord keeps you from all harm and watches over your life.
The Lord keeps watch over you as you come and go,
Both now and forever.

Psalms 121 (NLT)

Remember the earlier story of King David at Ziklag? Not one thing was lost although everything had been taken and was gone! David's situation went from burned to the ground, treasures, family and relationships ripped away, to the restoration of everything he had before, plus more. "Nothing was missing: young or old, boy or girl, plunder or anything else they had taken. David brought everything back" (1 Samuel 30:19 NLT). God is just waiting for your faith to rise up so He can do that for you!

"Let us hold unswervingly to the hope we profess, for He who promised is faithful" (Hebrews 10:23 KJV).

Afterward

It's been over a year since we completed our assignment to pray for Doug's restoration and breakthrough. God honored our prayers.

Doug is experiencing a resurgence of good health, new sources of financial stability and the beginning of family restoration. He has hope and is enjoying the favor of the Lord. Now, of course, like all of us, he is in the middle of a Covid 19 lockdown which affects all aspects of his life, just as it does each of us. God has planned good for each of us, and is waiting and watching and expecting to be merciful to us.

9 781973 697428